PRENTICE-HALL
FOUNDATIONS OF MODERN SOCIOLOGY SERIES

D0815018

PRENTICE-HALL
FOUNDATIONS OF MODERN SOCIOLOGY SERIES

Alex Inkeles, Editor

SOCIAL CHANGE

second edition
SOCIAL
CHANGE

WILBERT E. MOORE
University of Denver

Prentice-Hall, Inc., Englewood Cliffs, New Jersey

Library of Congress Cataloging in Publication Data

MOORE, WILBERT ELLIS.
  Social change.

  (Foundations of modern sociology series)
  Includes bibliographical references.
  1. Social change. I. Title.
HM101.M76 1974   301.24   73-13729
ISBN 0-13-815423-6
ISBN 0-13-815415-5 (pbk.)

Printed in the United States of America

10 9 8 7 6 5 4 3 2 1

Prentice-Hall International, Inc., London
Prentice-Hall of Australia, Pty. Ltd., Sydney
Prentice-Hall of Canada, Ltd., Toronto
Prentice-Hall of India Private Limited, New Delhi
Prentice-Hall of Japan, Inc., Tokyo

CONTENTS

PREFACE

Since the first edition of this small book appeared a great many books on social change have been published. I doubt that every piece of seemingly relevant literature has even come to my attention, for whether or not we are in the midst of an information explosion, we are certainly in the midst of a literature explosion. Aside from large numbers of rather tidy but inevitably constrained research studies in what I should summarily classify as "social psychology," my impression is that social change in its various aspects has received a disproportionate amount of published attention over the last several years. If my perception is correct, its implications are faintly amusing. In the first edition of *Social Change* I complained that the layman seemed more aware of change, and especially of turmoil, strife, and uncertainty, than did the "experts" on social organization and social process. I doubt that my complaint had anything to do with the ensuing flood of studies, but as a reader as well as writer I may be permitted to regret the torrent. I shall not attempt a "sociology of knowledge" interpretation of changing tastes in scholarly endeavors, for I find such interpretations often persuasive after the event and notably lacking in predictive propositions.

In presenting this revision I have attempted to be selectively attentive both to the critical comments that have appeared in the sociological literature, and to the new approaches that have appeared here and there. Yet I decided to keep the book short, for attention to the wealth of descriptive material (particularly relating to the difficulties in the modernization of newly developing countries) would have yielded an extremely long volume. Only length would make such a volume "monumental," for I see little that adds to our precise and general knowledge of patterned sequences. The studies of modernization, for example, still rely on the "comparative statics" of functional systems and thus lack time-ordered, causal relations.

A short book has certain advantages: most notably it must be unpretentious. It also has some disadvantages: references to descriptive and analytical studies must be selective and the selection may be thought arbitrary. Also, the exposition must be compact. I take some pride in clarity of exposition and even attribute to myself some occasional wit and grace in written style. But this is a book that cannot be readily skimmed by reading topic sentences or sub-heads and the reader is given little respite by way of repetition or illustration. In truth, I cannot find it in my heart to apologize for brevity.

I remain grateful to Harry H. Eckstein, Arnold S. Feldman, Mohammed Guessous, Marion J. Levy, Jr., and Norman B. Ryder for comments on the draft of the first edition. Professor Alex Inkeles invited me to write the book in the first place, encouraged this revision, and aided with cogent criticism.

By permission of the American Sociological Association I have drawn freely from my article "A Reconsideration of Theories of Social Change," published in the *American Sociological Review*, Vol. 25 (December 1960), pp. 810–15. I wish to thank the Association for this permission, and similarly thank the several other publishers who have permitted me to use short excerpts that are duly cited in footnote references. Here and there I have paraphrased materials from other recent publications of mine—I have "contributed" more than my share to the literature explosion—not always with scholarly citations. If one avoids infringing copyrights, invariably owned by others, self-theft strikes me as at worst a misdemeanor.

I repeat my concluding comment in the preface to the first edition, that, "I do accept complete responsibility for what is here presented, while secretly holding the view that my critics might share that responsibility just a little."

WILBERT E. MOORE

CHAPTER 1
THE NORMALITY
OF CHANGE

In these times scarcely a day passes without the newspaper and other mass media reporting a new or continuing crisis of grave international import in some little-known part of the world. The technology of communication and travel has "shrunken the size of the world." The politics of international tension have made that small world a dangerous place for human habitation.

The pace of change in general, and particularly the rate at which the world is becoming a single though highly disordered system, gives a kind of urgency to the notion that crisis is the ordinary state of social life. It would be false to argue that the contemporary condition of constant crisis is historically "normal," that men have "always" lived out their lives in a state of uncertainty not essentially different from the situation in which we find ourselves today. The contemporary world is more hazardous than the past, and the hazards affect more people. Social change, on the other hand, is not a uniquely modern phenomenon. Some kinds and degrees of change are universal in human experience. The speed of contemporary change is not totally illusory but it can be exaggerated, as when we pass a much slower-moving auto on the road and it seems to be standing still.

THE CONTEMPORARY CHAOS

By any crude measurement, the contemporary world appears to be changing more rapidly than at any time in human history, particularly if we accept an arbitrary division and define the contemporary period as the twentieth century. In fact, the early part of the century looks rather placid by comparison with the last few decades. Unless our vision is simply myopic and distorted, this strongly suggests that the rate of change is accelerating. And so it is.

This allegation is tenable only if the world setting is underscored. Wars and conquests, natural disaster, and social upheavals have occurred throughout recorded history, and there is no reason to suppose that prehistoric or non-literate peoples were exempt from radical dislocations. But in the modern world social change has taken on some special qualities and magnitudes.

Characteristics of Contemporary Change

The peculiar features of contemporary change may be summarized by a set of generalizations:

FOR ANY GIVEN SOCIETY or culture rapid change occurs frequently or "constantly."

CHANGES ARE NEITHER TEMPORALLY nor spatially isolated—that is changes occur in sequential chains rather than as "temporary" crises followed by quiet periods of reconstruction, and the consequences tend to reverberate through entire regions or virtually the entire world.

THUS, BECAUSE CONTEMPORARY CHANGE is probable "everywhere" and its consequences may be significant "everywhere," it has a dual basis.

THE PROPORTION OF CONTEMPORARY CHANGE that is either planned or issues from the secondary consequences of deliberate innovations is much higher than in former times.

ACCORDINGLY, THE RANGE OF MATERIAL technology and social strategies is expanding rapidly and the net effect is additive or cumulative despite the relatively rapid obsolescence of some procedures.

THE NORMAL OCCURRENCE of change affects a wider range of individual experience and functional aspects of societies in the modern world—not because such societies are in all respects more "integrated" but because virtually no feature of life is exempt from the expectation or normality of change.

Some Elements of Predictability and Uncertainty

The word "chaos" in our heading should not be taken too literally. Many features of social life persist from day to day and even from year to year. In terms of these *persistent patterns of action*, tomorrow will be about the same as today and yesterday, and next year will be about the same as this year and last. Many other features change, but in an orderly and thus fairly predictable way and amount. For these *trends* tomorrow will differ from today in about the degree that today differed from yesterday, and next year can be expected to prolong the trend established by previous annual comparisons. Some other elements of the future are predictable because the changes will be the product of *plans*, of deliberate intent and action. Even very rapid and complex changes have sources and consequences that are delimited rather than random, and therefore may be understood and predicted.

Yet if the contemporary world is not uniformly chaotic, there are complexities in social change that are likely to manifest themselves as *tensions and strains*. Persistent patterns in one field of action may eventually collide with trends in another—for example, the persistent pattern that impels nearly everyone to go to work at the same hour in the morning may be increasingly inconsistent with urban growth, the resulting strains being reflected in overloaded transportation facilities and traffic congestion. Trends that are relatively impervious to attempts to alter them may offset deliberate planning—for example, trends in birth rates may be out of phase with respect to plans for improving schools. Slow and simple changes may intersect with rapid and complex transformations—for example, the steady rate of economic growth through private investment may be inadequate to meet sudden and complex changes in national defense needs and foreign-aid policies.

Strains thus arise from lack of *synchronization* of types and rates of change. Uncertainty and lack of precise predictability arise from the *complexity of dynamic patterns*—that is, from a rather large "error" factor owing to the number and interplay of uncontrolled variables. The difficulty is in some measure intrinsic to the kinds of actions and events, of patterns and their alterations, with which we are dealing, for all science deals with standardized interrelations, with recurrent sequences, and has only a very limited capacity to predict unique combinations and events. An astronomer can predict the orderly relations among planets in a solar system, and the relations among such systems in a galaxy, but not the occurrence of a stellar explosion. Even variations in solar radiation are not precisely cyclical with regard to the earthly calculations of years, which is based precisely on another characteristic of the system, the orderly recurrence of the earth's migration around the sun. A physicist can formulate the general principle of gravitation, but cannot predict the behavior of a single atom. In order to forecast atomic behavior, he requires statistical probabilities based on large numbers. A human geneticist, by knowing the hereditary characteristics of an unborn child's parents and ancestors, can predict with some probability certain genetic traits and with fair confidence rule out others, but would not even consider an attempt to forecast the child's adult appearance or, for that matter with the current state of knowledge, its sex.

The Quest for Dynamic Laws

Part of the difficulty in predicting social change, however, is not intrinsic and ultimate, of a piece with "chance" events throughout nature and universe, but arises from ignorance of the possibly knowable. The reduction of ignorance and the consequent capacity to predict, if not control, the concatenation of events depend on careful observation and speculative thought, on continuous effort to bring order out of seeming chaos.

Because by definition the observation of change takes time, and because the complex interplay of factors requires a rather elaborate "intellectual model" for analysis, all scientific fields first develop an understanding of simple, *static* relationships. These relationships rest on co-existences repeatedly observed, but with each observation essentially photographic or "cross-sectional." Dynamic models and laws require knowledge of sequences of cause and effect in a temporal order. Simple and short-term relationships tend to be established before complex and long-term ones, and relationships observed under controlled, experimental conditions to precede relationships that occur "in nature."

Some of the nuances with respect to "static" and "dynamic" principles can be illustrated from the study of astronomy. Many carefully recorded observations, plus the integrative capacity of several brilliant theoretical minds, went into the theory that explains the orderly interdependence and movements of planets of our solar system.[1] Yet that system is essentially "functional," the cycles neatly recurrent and the longest one requiring only a few earth-years to run its course. The impressive manner in which scientists predicted the position of unseen planets was, however, a static prediction, based on the characteristics of the visible system and the components "necessary" in order to complete an orderly picture of its operation. A truly dynamic theory of the solar system, to say nothing of the universe, is very much lacking. That is to say, there is no commonly accepted and moderately verifiable formulation that is concerned with changes in the system itself, its history, and its destiny.

The evolution of our contemporary scientific understanding of the solar system occurred over many centuries,[2] but that passage of time is

---

1. Thomas S. Kuhn, *The Copernican Revolution* (Cambridge: Harvard University Press, 1957).

2. Ibid.

somewhat misleading. Prior to Newton's time astronomers devoted relatively little time to observations of the solar system or to formulating observationally based theories about it. Today, however, we allocate time and resources freely to the pursuit of increased knowledge. Although time can never be a long-run substitute for intelligence, there is some prospect that both time and intelligence will now and in the future be devoted to the subjects of theoretical as well as practical interest, including the course of man's own changing destiny.

The present, then, is characterized by a much greater degree of change than was the past, and some of the changes in magnitude—for example, in the emphasis now placed on problem solving and planning—are so great as to suggest changes in kind. The distinction is not terribly important, for novelty is rarely rootless and total, exhibiting no elements of continuity with antecedent conditions. And social change as such is not a peculiarly modern phenomenon. It is the intent of this book to underscore the normality of change as well as its special contemporary characteristics and magnitudes, to explore causes and directions, and to establish such a measure of understandable order as our present knowledge and thinking permit.

ORDER AND CHANGE

Many of the significant components of man's social existence are persistent even if examined over considerable periods of time. The daily, weekly, and annual schedules of man's activities show a remarkable consistency, as do the forms and patterns that deal with life's major events, such as birth, marriage, and death. The persistence of patterns gives order and constancy to recurrent events. In terms of behavior, many elements of persistence are more nearly cyclical, the near repetition of sequences of action over various time periods.[3] If we analyze these, we see that even order is marked by change from moment to moment, and persistence is the characteristic of the pattern, of the *system* of action, but not of single actions. Other elements of persistence are not so narrowly timed, but are exhibited "on occasion," such as the prescribed rational and ritual procedures attendant on transitions in life-stages. These patterns are marked by two components of change: the moment-to-moment sequence of prescribed actions, and the differences in behavior before and after the transition. Yet still the pattern persists.

We come therefore to an important distinction: that between mere sequences of small actions, which essentially *comprise* the pattern, and

---

3.   See Wilbert E. Moore, *Man, Time, and Society* (New York: Wiley, 1963), Chap. 2, "The Temporal Location of Activities."

changes in the system itself. Changes in the system may take the form of alterations in tempo, boundaries, the internal rules of conduct, or the relation of the particular system to its environment.

This is a distinction that may have to be made more than once in any analysis of order and change, since the system that is the focus of attention may be very.simple or extremely complex. The concept of "system" is applicable to any situation in which units are interrelated long enough or regularly enough to be observed A social system requires that the units be persons—more properly, *actors* or *role-players*—whose interaction is governed by rules or *norms*. Particular systems may be organized as groups, which then take on such additional characteristics as collective goals or *values*. The units of larger systems may in fact be aggregates of actors who thus constitute sub-systems. And here is the source of the difficulty in analyzing order and change or any other characteristic of patterned behavior: Care must be taken to identify the system that is under analysis, for like Joshua's vision there are wheels within wheels. We are not told of that vision whether the wheels were connected and synchronized, but we do know that in complex systems the parts often have considerable autonomy and independent variability.

The persistent and repetitive character of many aspects of social behavior gives a kind of "static predictability" to human life and thus makes it tolerable. There appear to be psychological limits to people's tolerance for chaos—and, incidentally, limits to their tolerance for endless repetition.[4]

Orderly persistence and the "systemic" qualities of life in human aggregates are also significant for a broad area of social science. A great deal of sociological (or economic or political) theory is based on answers to the question, "What patterns of action coexist and how are they interrelated?" Such "static" propositions are by no means inconsequential. Indeed it is doubtful that the understanding of change—detecting orderly properties in the transformations of behavior patterns or social structures—would be possible without an underlying basis of persistence and regularity.

Backgrounds of Contemporary Theory

Many earlier theories of society that claimed to be scientific were in fact theories of change. They sought to explain the present in terms of the past. Comte,[5] the French sociologist who coined the term "sociology," saw civilization as starting with a "theological" stage in which

---

4. Sylvan Tomkins, *Affect-Imagery-Consciousness*, Vol. I (New York: Springer, 1962), Chap. 3, "Amplification, Attention, and Affects."

5. Auguste Comte, *Cours de Philosophie Positive* (Paris: Rouen, 1830–1842).

the explanations of all things and events were supernatural, passing through a "metaphysical" stage in which abstract conceptions and reasons were the basic explanatory principles, and finally, reaching a "positivistic" stage in which both nature and society would be understood and ordered on the basis of scientific study.

Following the publication of Darwin's revolutionary idea of biological evolution, the notion of extending evolutionary principles to account for changes in societies and differentiation among them became very popular. The British anthropologists and sociologists Morgan,[6] Tyler[7] and Spencer[8] were substantially influenced by Darwin's theories. Yet the social evolutionists fell out of favor rapidly, partly because they tried to order the extreme diversity of contemporary non-literate and advanced societies into a single evolutionary scale according to stages. Moreover, most of their evidence was too contemporary and essentially cross-sectional. Even when the evidence was historical, the period represented was relatively short in evolutionary terms. The rumored death of evolutionary doctrine was grossly exaggerated or at least premature, as its relatively recent revival testifies. That revival, which will be discussed in the concluding chapter, is marked by disavowing claims to account for all significant diversity and all significant change.

Once the notion that contemporary "primitive" societies could be taken as equivalent to early stages of "civilized" societies was seriously challenged, the evidence for long-term evolutionary change of particular societies or cultures became extremely thin. Archaeology had not in the late nineteenth century, and still has not, provided a very extensive prehistoric base for social change, and it is unlikely to do so in any direct way. The essential features of social systems—patterns of action and constellations of beliefs and rules of conduct—are not such as to leave archaeological remains. They must be inferred from remnants of so-called material culture: tools, containers, and weapons; types of dwellings; evidences of use of fire; and perhaps kinds of food. Reconstructing cultures or societies from pottery shards and flakes of flint paradoxically requires reading backward from contemporary or historically recorded evidence concerning the kinds of social structures likely to be associated with particular material products of human action.

Early in this century some scholars[9] began to advocate abandon-

---

6. Lewis Henry Morgan, *Ancient Society* (New York: Holt, 1877).

7. Edward B. Tyler, *Primitive Culture*, 3rd American ed. (New York: Holt, 1889).

8. Herbert Spencer, *First Principles* (New York: Appleton, 1890); also his *Principles of Sociology*, 3 vols. (New York: Appleton, 1898–1899).

9. Albion W. Small, for example, in articles in the early volumes of the *American Journal of Sociology*.

ing the "fruitless quest for origins," on grounds that were essentially what would now be called "functionalistic"; that is, that social behavior and various items of culture could be understood only within their setting or context, and not by the vain attempt to seek their first appearance.

Although the systemic qualities of social life were not denied nor totally neglected by earlier theorists, it remained for such functionalists as Radcliffe-Brown[10] and Malinowski,[11] both British social anthropologists, to formalize certain methodological assumptions into a kind of doctrine. One of the most significant of these assumptions was that any item or component of the system (say a society or culture) could be explained in terms of the system as a whole. Thus, to take a seemingly trivial but actually fairly challenging example, the buttons on men's jacket sleeves should not be explained by tracing their origin to the fastening of armored gauntlets in Medieval Europe but simply in terms of the functions of conventional style. The notion of a "survival" of a functionless form was rejected and replaced by the notion that forms would survive only if they were related to the system's operation.

A concern for both history and the future was by no means lost to the sociological tradition by the seeming ascendancy of functionalism. The influence of Marx's conception of dialectical processes, producing an inherent dynamics in societies,[12] was not entirely lost in political turmoil. Other than as a target for critical attack, however, Marxist theories were long subordinated or simply neglected in the primary focus of social scientists (anthropologists, economists, political scientists, and sociologists) on less grand themes, indeed on detailed and primarily contemporary observation.

THE AMENDMENT
OF FUNCTIONAL THEORIES

As some of the functionalist assumptions were more fully developed and made more explicit they began to be challenged and amended,[13]

10. A. R. Radcliffe-Brown, *Structure and Function in Primitive Society* (London: Cohen, 1952).

11. Bronislaw Malinowski, "Culture," in *Encyclopedia of the Social Sciences* (New York: Macmillan, 1930). (Vol. IV in 1930 ed.; Vol. II in 1937 ed.)

12. See Karl Marx, *A Contribution to the Critique of Political Economy*, trans. by N. I. Stone (Chicago: Charles H. Kerr, 1904). See also Robert A. Nisbet, *Social Change and History* (New York: Oxford University Press, 1969), pp. 171–72, 177–78.

13. See Robert K. Merton, "Manifest and Latent Functions," in his *Social Theory and Social Structure*, rev. ed. (Glencoe, Ill.: Free Press, 1957), Chap. 1.

and in some cases extended. These challenges and modifications have had an important bearing on the problems of social change.

The functionalist assumption that has been most severely challenged but that still exhibits a hardy power of survival in one form or another involves the "integration" of social systems. In its most extreme form, the assumption could be expressed as "what is, must be." Criticized by Professor Pitirim Sorokin as "functional teleogy,"[14] this notion that "everything works out for the best in the best of all possible worlds" has been generally rejected with theoretically important results:

SOCIAL SYSTEMS, and particularly large-scale ones such as entire societies, exhibit inconsistent and discordant elements.

THUS THE RELATION OF AN ELEMENT to a system is not necessarily "eufunctional"; that is, it does not necessarily contribute to the continuity or survival of the system. It may be "disfunctional"; that is, it may contribute to the disruption or eventual destruction of the system.[15] It is, indeed, even possible that an element within a system may have *no* significant consequences.

BECAUSE OF UNCERTAIN BUT LATENT RELATIONS within systems, particular elements may be eufunctional for part of the system and disfunctional for the over-all system. For example, the code of "honor among thieves" serves professional criminals better than it does the maintenance of a society's legal codes.

THE RELATION BETWEEN FORM AND FUNCTION is neither random nor precise. The principle of "structural suitability" is always subject to a possible modification in terms of "structural substitutability." For example, utility does not demand that men's jackets come adorned with buttons. Less trivially, an industrialized economy does not *require* a parliamentary democracy.

THE FACT OF SURVIVAL provides an inferential, but not conclusive, test of suitability in view of the possible looseness and discontinuities of social systems.

From Functionalism to Dynamics

The introduction of the idea that elements of social systems had "survival value" for the system had interesting and important consequences. Implicitly at least the idea of survival indicated that some form of selectivity occurred, with disfunctional or irrelevant patterns being dropped and useful patterns persisting. Since such selectivity could only take place over a considerable span of time, systems must change

14. For reference to Sorokin's criticism, see Marion J. Levy, Jr., *The Structure of Society* (Princeton: Princeton University Press, 1952), pp. 52–53.

15. Ibid.

through time. Thus a seemingly static theory became in fact a dynamic one.

Functionalism has been extended to the attempt to identify the "functional requisites of any society."[16] By this view certain kinds of social action—for example, legitimate reproduction, socialization of the young in terms of both education and acceptance of moral precepts and maintenance of order—must be performed if any society is going to operate as a system and persist through time. The functional requisites provide a key to the *common* structural features of society, since the patterns of action and forms of social organization must be suitable. Thus functionalism in this form provides the basis of essentially static generalizations about human societies. This approach, however, also reintroduces an implicitly evolutionary notion, since the presumption is that various social systems have failed to persist for want of some requisite function.

Yet most sociological propositions are relational or correlational. The fact that sociologists have directed their attention primarily to the orderly characteristics of social systems has had the unnecessary but real consequence of distracting their interest from intrinsic sources of change. Thus change in the sense of alterations in systems rather than repetitive sequences is often viewed as an unexplained external variable, significant only in its systemic consequences. The view that society is comprised of functionally interdependent units provides, of course, an excellent basis for an orderly and coherent analysis and account of the result of given changes. It does not always provide an adequate basis for predicting change, or even for explaining it in a general or "lawful" and not simply historical or unique way.

Some of the potential mischief derives from the concept of a social system as in "equilibrium"—that is, in a steady state owing to the balance of complementary forces. Now an equilibrium model can be as useful as any theoretical tool that asks how "nature" would look if it followed the characteristics of the artificially created order. All analytical sciences use such models, for they afford investigators a way of abstracting and generalizing, a way of selecting relevant phenomena from the irrelevant. Yet all models provoke some questions and inhibit others, and the inhibited questions may prove to be interesting from other points of view.

The equilibrium version of systems analysis either forecloses questions about the sources of change, or if discordant internal elements are brought into the analysis, the theoretical model will predict one direction of change, and one only—change that restores the system to a steady state.

Social systems do indeed exhibit persistent patterns and comple-

16.   Ibid., Chap. 4.

mentary functions. Specialization, for example, "requires" coordinating differentiated activities, including some way of exchanging goods or services among the specialized producers. An equilibrium model is perfectly appropriate for the kind of generalized statement about the interdependence of structural variables (specialization, coordination, exchange) that we have just made. It would be impossible from such a model to predict an initial change in any of the variables. If such a change were observed, or imagined for purposes of theoretical analysis, the model would predict only such other complementary changes as would restore the equilibrium.

Society as a Tension-Management System[17]

The view of society as a tension-management rather than as a self-equilibrating system has distinct advantages in making *both* order and change problematical, but also "normal." Tensions—or inconsistencies and strains, if the word "tensions" is too subjective or has too psychological a connotation—are intrinsic to social systems, not simply accidental accompaniments or the product of changes that impinge on the system from external sources. Once the tensions characteristic of all or of particular types of social systems are identified, they are predicted to be the probable sites of change. Now, as an equilibrium model would indicate, the predicted change may well reduce the strain. And the postulate that social action is interconnected—that it is to be analyzed in terms of a system—permits hypotheses to be formulated concerning the effects of particular changes, the secondary consequences, including those that come full circle and make additional alterations in the original tension point. Yet the theoretical tension-management model differs from the presumption of equilibrium in several significant respects:

> TO THE DEGREE that at least some tensions are really intrinsic, and not simply organizational problems that can be readily resolved, the predicted change will neither restore an equilibrium or static state nor create a new one.

> THE CONSEQUENCES OF CHANGE will almost certainly be tension-producing as well as possibly tension-reducing.

> THE USE OF THE TERM "TENSION" does not imply that change will initially reduce tension. For some sequential analyses it may be appropriate to identify or predict tension-producing changes rather than change-producing tensions, not to evade the postulate of intrinsic tensions, but rather

17. See Wilbert E. Moore and Arnold S. Feldman, "Society as a Tension-Management System," in George Baker and Leonard S. Cottrell, Jr. (eds.), *Behavioral Science and Civil Defense Disaster Research Group*, Study No. 16 (Washington: National Academy of Sciences, National Research Council, 1962), pp. 93–105.

to take into account the necessity for a starting point and the frequent desirability of "getting particular," of making rather specific predictions rather than highly general ones. For example, there is an intrinsic tension between any social system that endures beyond the lifetime of its members or the age limits of membership, and the system's mode of recruiting new members. Here, then, is a likely place to look for change. The analysis may begin, however, by identifying a change in the number or qualities of recruits and then predicting the tensions that the change can be expected to produce.

THE CONCEPTION OF SOCIETY (or any social structure) as a tension-management system involves no presumption at all that the management is "successful," or that the system as identified in fact persists, or even that it will last long enough to permit us to speak of "transitions" from one system to another. The probability of any of those things happening can be determined only by identifying the system and the variables that will determine the course of its change. One possible course may be destruction.

THE UBIQUITY OF CHANGE

Once we have arrived at the point where we can speak systematically about social change, where we can regard at least some of the changes in people's lives, in groups, and in entire societies as possibly regular or lawful, then we can see change virtually everywhere we turn. Of course this situation comes about in part because of the especially changeful character of the contemporary world. But if we ask of historical materials what changes took place, or if we put the same question to ethnographic descriptions of non-literate societies prior to substantial Western influence, it turns out that some sources and forms of change are indeed universal.

Within an individual's own experience, the most certain and most universal change is associated with his life cycle. Man shares mortality with all living creatures, but many of his experiences prior to death are peculiar to his species. He goes through a long period of "infancy" marked both by physical growth and, most importantly, by learning and becoming *socialized* to the various norms and role requirements that membership in his social system entails. Various stages in the life cycle may be marked off clearly, and the transition may be symbolized by a public ritual (a *rite de passage*[18]). Or the stages may be rather hazy yet still significant for changing role requirements and role relationships. Thus we expect older people to "slow down," although they may reach a sharply defined stage of old age only when they retire, if at all. Sim-

---

18. See Arnold Van Gennep, *Les Rites de Passage* (Paris: Nouvy, 1909). See also Moore, *Man, Time, and Society*, Chap. 3, "The Ordering of Individual Lives."

ilarly, failure to "act one's age" brings censure, although the age boundaries that may have been transgressed may be fuzzy.

Of course the life-cycle experiences of individuals may be considered as another example of sequential action, although a long-term
one, repeated from one person to another, and even from one generation
to another without essentially altering the *social* system, a mere changing
of actors in a drama with an unchanging plot. And so it may be, particularly if we want to limit our interest to major system changes. At a
finer or more subtle level of analysis, however, the various aspects of
socialization are quite unlikely to be endlessly and precisely repetitive
and stable. The individual passes through a *succession* of positions and
corresponding roles. For the social system of which he is a part, a succession of role-players maintains the underlying order. Yet the correspondence between individual and pattern is always incomplete, the
socialization of the individual at least faintly imperfect. Mere *succession*
causes change, however small.

Flexibilities in the System

Let us look at the minimum "flexibilities" that enable social systems to endure the phenomena of succession. If we start, say, with seemingly standardized adult role requirements, differentiated perhaps only
according to age, sex, and position in a kinship system, it will be apparent
at once that the several or successive persons that observe the same role
requirements will not be in all respects alike. Some will be stockier, or
stronger, or more vigorous than others; some will be more intelligent;
others will differ in the way these and other physiological and partly
hereditary traits have interacted with their social experiences.

Role requirements are thus likely to constitute ranges of tolerable
behavior rather than highly precise behavioral limitations. Extremes will
normally be subject to negative sanctions, with considerable latitude in
between. The most elaborate system of positional specialization wherein
expected performance is precisely specified is to be found in the large
"bureaucracy" or administrative organzation, and even that type of organization is somewhat affected by personnel succession.

Any enduring system, then, must have some degree of flexibility in
exacting compliance from its members, and this flexibility in turn provides the possibility and indeed the probability of innovation, however
modest that may be.

The probability of innovation is enhanced by another source of
flexibility at which we have already hinted. A society or any part of it
that recruits new members as infants must impart to them appropriate
knowledge and skills, and must see to it that they "internalize" the
values and moral codes that the society deems important. The combined

process of formal education and moral internalization is called *socialization*. Yet despite its essentially integrative character, socialization is an additional source of uncertainty in social systems.

To say that children are born into society or culture is elliptical. They are normally born into a family unit, which in turn can be expected to be only partially representative of a generalized and uniform set of values and normative and cognitive orientations. The universality of social differentiation structurally precludes exact uniformity in family position. Even when they occupy similar positions in the social structure, it is extremely unlikely that families will follow exactly uniform patterns of child care and rearing, or indeed that the same family will exhibit uniform behavior in the intimate interaction with successive offspring. Thus biological differences interact with diverse personality and structural factors to provide a rather wide range of possible variation. On a strictly actuarial view of socialization, uniformities are somewhat more remarkable than variations.

If adult social positions are not greatly differentiated, if adult destination can be largely foretold for infants at birth, and if adult models are constantly at hand for children to emulate or to shun, then social control of relatively helpless infants may indeed produce a system that is somewhat self-sustaining. Besides the uncertainties arising from what might be called "individual differences," however, there are two other manifestations of structural variability and uncertainty that we should examine. Both derive from the bio-social facts of social recruitment by biological reproduction and the uncertain life span of any given individual.

It is extremely doubtful that any society ever existed, and certainly none has ever been observed, in which the rate of reproduction, its distribution by sex, and the rate of survival at least until early adulthood has produced a precise and continuous numerical duplication of the population. Even where infanticide has been practiced as a kind of social corrective to biological error, its aim has been qualitative—the elimination of the deformed or apparent weaklings—or an attempt to alter the survival ratio of the sexes (usually to reduce the number of females) but not to prevent a change in population as such.

The social sciences have commonly treated population changes as essentially biological variables, external to social systems. Although this view is wrong in many particulars, it remains true that a precise total and differential control of fertility and mortality is extremely unlikely. Thus the exact size of a population cannot be expected to remain stationary through time, and it is even less likely that births and deaths will exactly maintain existing distributions among various social categories. Some kinship groups are likely to expand and others to contract.

A ruling elite or an hereditary priesthood may be over-supplied with people to place, and some classes of artisans may be faced with recruiting youngsters from other groups.

If the numerical duplication of adult roles is not in fact assured by precise fertility controls, then one of the crucial requisites for a relatively untroubled socialization process is missing, for the adult destinies of children must differ in some measure from those prevailing at any given time.

Survival uncertainties also are an added source of variability. Replacement rates for relatively fixed and numerically precise positions will be affected by the longevity of incumbents, as will the supply of potential successors. Some men, for example, may never become family "patriarchs" because they are outlived by a predecessor, and others find themselves "elder statesmen" at early ages. Given the high mortality rates generally characteristic exactly of those tribal societies commonly depicted as unchanging, and if our argument with regard to the effects of succession is valid, the rate of succession alone should lead us to expect at least moderate fluctuations in patterns and relationships.

There is an extension of this line of reasoning that is also worth mentioning. With high mortality rates, elaborate kinship systems are more likely to be ideal than actual, for the simple reason that there is a high probability that death will have left many nominal kinship positions unfilled. The implication of this circumstantial argument is that if kinship role requirements are really mandatory, and not simply contingent on the availability of role-players, additional duties will devolve on substitute kinsmen. This problem is readily and nearly universally recognized as applicable to the widowed parent. An extended kinship system, entailing a great many distinct positions, increases the probability that some positions will be filled by substitutes, if they are filled at all. It must also be expected that a "mandatory" marriage system that radically restricts the determination of socially suitable mates would leave a significant portion of the young adults unmarried and presumably childless. At the very least this would impair the "normality" of marriage and parenthood and suggest the high probability that actual behavior will be evasive of ideal norms. Thus again we find a basis in the characteristics of societies for supposing that their social arrangements must be subject to change.

Now where does this leave us with regard to the probability of change in societies that have an essentially "hereditary" system of social succession? We have argued that individual differences, complicated by differences in socialization, will prevent an exact and persistent duplication of role performances. We have also argued that variations in fertility and mortality will in time affect even the number and numerical distribution of actual adult positions. These variations led us to note the importance of turnover rate in leading to changing performances and the necessity of altering role expectations because of an over-suppy or under-supply of ideal candidates. Incidentally, the seeming simplicity of being socialized to a position in a kinship structure is revealed to be an over-simplification on two counts:

> 1.   The role requirements expected of any individual in a kinship system are multiple not singular, and are most numerous exactly in situations where kinship is a predominant element in the social system generally;
> 2.   Uncertainties in recruitment and succession make actual role requirements also somewhat uncertain.

Once we accept the fact that social fluctuations, variations, and uncertainties are characteristic of societies everywhere, then we can entertain a further hypothetical possibility. This possibility is that some sub-systems may be relatively autonomous with regard to other parts of the social order and are perhaps subject to fluctuations or trends that are neither causes nor consequences of changes in other parts of the system. For example—and these are merely hypothetical illustrations at this point—the types of military formations may change more rapidly than the technology of agricultural production in the same society, and continue to do so over very long periods; instruments endowed with sacred significance may be relatively impervious to merely utilitarian improvement, but theological views of the cosmos may be more open to discussion and evolution than mundane theories of human nature; decorative forms and modes of aesthetic expression may be scarcely affected by changes in such major functional institutions as marriage or government, and conversely may change by a kind of autonomous evolution with little effect on the more "practical" aspects of social existence.

To some degree, then, it appears that the fairly standard view that non-literate and peasant or agrarian societies prior to relatively recent times were marred by little social change is subject to substantial suspicion. The possibility of error is increased by two other circumstances, one theoretical, one methodological. The "functional equilibrium model" of societies or cultures has provoked questions relating to the interdependence of roles and patterns and norms and values, but not questions about inconsistencies and strains and variations through time. Armed with this kind of intellectual equipment, the field worker has studied "his" tribe or village fairly intensively but also fairly briefly and has thus tended to record and interpret his snapshot but not to see or be able to see the changes in the system arising from sources other than the contaminating influence of contemporary contact with the modern Western World.

The Magnitude of Change

Were the flexibilities and uncertainties inherent in all social systems the only universal sources of change, their relative neglect in contemporary sociological theory would not be of crucial signifiance. Short-term cycles such as mark the daily or weekly or annual round of activities may be viewed as the changeful way in which stable systems are maintained. Life cycles may be equally inconsequential for alterations in values, norms, and positions that characterize social systems. Even the small-scale fluctuations in the way roles are performed and in the numerical distribution of role-players for standardized positions may not have any substantial significance for the enduring qualities of systems or the efficacy with which, on balance, they perform whatever functions they must in order to persist. In other words, the arguments we have so far advanced for expecting structural changes to be universal may be a valid attention to detail, while having little significance for the "big picture."

Viewed in this light, the changes that alter the detailed way in which systems operate but that scarcely affect the magnitude or direction of these changes have more effect on the theoretical model of a "social structure" than on a "dynamic" model for changing systems. Variations and uncertainties would thus impair our ability to make predictions on the basis of a static empirical model, without aiding us in predicting the course of enduring structural changes.

It appears that major changes in the magnitude or direction of societies may be very slow in developing and perhaps not become apparent for generations. Yet fluctuations and flexibilities are important for major change, for they establish a significant *condition* for consequential change, if not its source.

Were we to take seriously the "perfectly integrated" equilibrated model of social systems, any change would be either trivial or tragic: trivial because it would be quickly suppressed and rectified or tragic because every characteristic of the system would be altered by any enduring change within it. We have seen that this model has serious shortcomings, and this dilemma clearly leads to another. The looser, more variable, and strain-ridden model we have adopted leaves open the possibility, adequately confirmed by direct and inferential evidence, that many changes are neither trivial nor tragic. What remains is to show how these intrinsic flexibilities in social systems provide the appropriate environment for changes. These changes are properly attributable to the system itself and not simply to the detailed way in which it operates.

The first point to be noted about flexibilities in systems is that they are limited, and the limits are of course most readily apparent in cases of conspicuous failure. Some examples are in order.

A single person improperly socialized may still be induced to conform by the use of external rewards and punishments. Indeed, virtually all individuals may be primarily constrained rather than conscientious in some aspects of their behavior as long as most people conscientiously comply in most situations. The exact tolerance limits for conformity may not be very precise, and are most easily discerned at the extremes. We can demolish the kind of "hedonistic" view that men behave only in terms of self-interest without regard to conscience by first considering all its implications. By this view, all social conformity would be the consequence of the rewards and punishments assigned by "others." But who are these others, and why do they impose the rules of conduct? By following this argument we finally encounter the classic question, *Quis custodiet ipsos custodes*, who guards the guardians? If values and rules of conduct are to persist, someone must believe in them, and unless the belief in them is very general the "administrative" costs of constant surveillance and of the imposition of control by terror will be very high—a drain on scarce time and energy that would otherwise be available for other objectives. Thus if the socialization process breaks down, and particularly if as a result of the breakdown, values and standards of conduct arise that are different from those that are officially sanctioned and imposed, the system will change either by being overthrown or by significantly altering its social control. Some conditions that, in turn, might produce results that would breach the tolerance limits for maintaining the system will be discussed in due course.

Similar hazardous and system-changing extremes readily come to mind, particularly those involving the fluctuations in population size and distribution. Even a turnover in population may have critical consequences if, for example, it outstrips the recruitment and training of new members and yokes the society with many incompetent or uncommitted performers.

Thus an extremely high rate of change in otherwise minor fluctuations may have major consequences. Also when a form of change normally marked by "fluctuations" persists without changing direction, it will force a change in a system. With respect to population growth over the short run for most areas of the world and for most periods of history, demographic imbalances probably have resulted in "fluctuations" and adjustments. Over the long run it appears clear that human populations have grown, although most rapidly in the modern era. Persistent growth, then, has changed not only the size of social systems, by definition, but also the complexity and interrelationships or organizational forms within systems, usually with accompanying strains. Thus a form of variability within systems has become an authentic source of significant change.[19]

Unattained Ideals

Is there, however, a source or are there sources of changes in systems, whether the changes are universal and not merely repetitive, trivial, "minor" fluctuations, or essentially unpredictable accidents? The affirmative answer lies in a universal feature of human societies which in its most general form may be stated as the *lack of close correspondence between the "ideal" and the "actual"* in many pervasive contexts of social behavior.

There are two aspects of this universal source of strain and change in social systems, although all analytic separations are subject to contamination in that we *are* dealing with systems. Those two aspects of the relation between the ideal and the actual are:

1. The ubiquity of the "environmental challenge," and
2. The ubiquity of non-conformity and of failure to achieve ideal values.

Let us discuss and explain these two aspects in somewhat more detail. First, we shall look at the phrase, "The ubiquity of the environmental challenge." Man is, among other things, a biological creature living in a partially non-human environment, to which he must "adjust," although that adjustment may include domination, control, or destruction. The consequences of his actions on "nature" may also affect his continued capacity to survive or control, with no automatic assurance that all his efforts will have benign results. A fashionable distinction has been drawn between primitive man as a slave of nature and modern man as its master. Both pictures are clearly overdrawn, although there are substantial differences in understanding, predicting, and controlling the non-human elements and events. The non-literate food-gatherer's capacity to identify edible flora and fauna and the professional meteorologist's meager capacity to predict the weather and negligible ability to control it, warn against too extreme a distinction.

By identifying man's relations with his environment as a universal source of change we are not surreptitiously introducing an external "environmentalist" cause of change. The difficulties with that view may be succinctly summarized:

19. See Kingsley Davis, *Human Society* (New York: Macmillan, 1949), Chap. 20.

CLIMATIC TRENDS, physiographic features, and biological characteristics change very slowly relative to the social dynamics for which causes are sought. A constant cannot explain a variable in any system of logic.

ALTHOUGH ENVIRONMENTAL CHANGE will indeed have social consequences, the purity of the causal direction is spurious. Human activity alters climate, topography, and even human biology. The contemporary "ecology movement" and other manifestations of concern for environmental alterations have been provoked precisely by the impairment and destruction of various "natural balances" through shortsighted human intervention. Nor will biological determinism withstand scrutiny. "Natural selection" in the human species is always "social selection." Population changes are caused by characteristics of patterned human activity as well as having consequences for social systems.

THUS THE RELEVANCE OF HUMAN HEREDITY and the non-human environment is always conditional and relative to the technology, social organization, and cultural values of human societies.[20]

What we are asserting is that there is no reason to suppose that "culture" and "setting" are ever in perfect adjustment. From the most elementary kinds of strain produced by demographic imbalances, the hazards of life in the seen and unseen environment, the level of sustenance and physical comfort to the much more complex and interactive relation between technological man and an altered environment that contains old and new lethal hazards,[21] man has neither solved the problem of mortality nor a host of subsidiary but refractory problems of living in peaceful command of the universe. And anything less than total control of human biology and the non-human environment leaves ample opportunities for strain and innovation.

The other ubiquitous source of change-producing strain arises from the inherent fact that social order is a moral order and from the associated fact that non-conformity to this moral order occurs in all societies. The ideal values are not generally achieved, and prescriptions governing conduct are never consistent. Ideal norms that are logically contradictory can be found in all cultures. More importantly, roles collide in particular contexts of social behavior. Ambivalence and ambiguity are intrinsic to the human condition.

These vicissitudes occur in part precisely because of the uncertainties and flexibility in social systems and in part because human behavior is goal-directed and human societies are committed to values as well as organized around conventional procedures that make orderly interaction

20. See Wilbert E. Moore, "Introduction" in Wilbert E. Moore (ed.), *Technology and Social Change*, (Chicago: Quadrangle, 1972).

21. See Rachel Carson, *The Silent Spring* (Boston: Houghton Mifflin, 1962); Lewis Mumford, *The Myth of the Machine*, II, *The Pentagon of Power* (New York: Harcourt, Brace & Jovanovich, 1970), especially Chap. 11, "The Megatechnic Wasteland."

feasible. Ideals not achieved are not thereby ineffective, mere vague vapor-
ings of the human imagination. Were they of no consequence, their removal or radical alteration would have no effect on people's behavior nor
on the orderly patterns of social existence. Such situations are extremely
rare. Usually the inconsistency between the ideal and the actual is tension-
producing and hospitable to change. Overt violation of prevalent practices must somehow be dealt with, for it genuinely challenges the persistence of morally supported standards. Widespread recognition that
human performance falls short of perfection may lead to the acceptance
of more "realistic" standards, but this development is itself a significant
change. Recent manifestations of changing moral standards among
youths, and their partial or grumbling acceptance by older adults, remind us that even ideal norms are subject to change. Note also, however,
that many of the youngsters complained of the hypocrisy of merely verbal
adherence to older conventional values. Equally instructive has been
the reassertion of some ideal values: equal justice for the poor, democratic determination of policies, building better societies.

We are now in a position to link the flexibilities inherent in social
systems and the existence of environmental and social challenges. The
one provides for "chance" variability and the other provides for selective
adaptation. We shall discuss these two basic postulates in evolutionary
theory at greater length in the final chapter. Together they enable us to
predict *cumulative change*: for example, in technology narrowly con-
strued as the ways of dealing with the non-human environment, and in
the forms of social organization and social control that are responsive to
the problems both of the criminal minority and of the imperfect majority.

Reciting resistances to innovation has been the stock in trade of
dedicated "functional" theorists in sociology and anthropology owing in
large measure to the dictates of a theoretical model that exaggerated the
intricate integration of systems and thus could view significant change
only as tragic from the point of view of orderly continuity. We have now
laid both the factual and theoretical basis for the proposition that in addition to "trivial" changes that do not essentially alter the system, and
genuinely threatening changes that may well be resisted and suppressed,
there are likely to be forms of selective adaptation with significant and
enduring consequences.

The view of the mindless character of change, particularly in prehistoric and non-literate societies, is possibly patronizing. Our earlier
reference to "chance" variability was at that point avoiding issues, since
many of the sources and varieties of change are not really by chance.
The emphasis on a kind of random variability and accidental survival
has been mainly directed at overcoming a "rationalistic" bias in older
interpretations of origins. It is easy to be humorously critical of the picture of a group of elders sitting 'round the campfire deciding to end the

state of nature in which life was "solitary, poor, nasty, brutish, and short,[22] by inventing a polity complete with a sovereign, or their counterparts deciding to invent the "incest taboo" for reasons of eugenics or the hopeless tangle in kinship identification and terminology; or still another group who vote to establish a prize and exclusive patent protection for the person who would invent the wheel.

Yet the opposite extreme of fatalistic acceptance of life's hazards and man's evil ways is, on careful consideration, no more persuasive. It is extremely improbable that a fatalistic system of "operational philosophy" (that is, the explanatory theory guiding the ordinary run of men) was ever completely institutionalized. The organization and institutionalization of change, making constructive innovation a moral virtue, is rare and mostly modern, it is true. Yet to attribute problem-solving ability and planned improvements only to modern man, and to make the distinction between contemporary purpose and ancient accident dichotomous, may be as false as all other dichotomies. Man has sometimes been characterized, with patent technological bias, as the "tool-using animal." It seems more consistent with humanity as well as, incidentally, more accurate, to call him the "problem-solving animal."

Man's wisdom as well as his mundane behavior is somewhat short of divine perfection, however, and the selective adaptation of systems and the selective adoption of changes are by no means uniformly benign in their long-term results. Men have wastefully fished out their food-producing waters or killed off their life-sustaining supplies of game. They have invented forms of social suppression that degraded the masters as surely as they degraded the slaves. Modern man has indeed developed the arts of self-destruction to a high degree and with astonishing speed. He has here and there dumped the rich top soil produced by the ages into the sea within a generation, and polluted his air and water and food with lethally invisible natural and unnatural hazards. He has invented ideologies that approximate the counter-utopian society depicted by George Orwell's *1984*,[23] wherein war is peace and slavery is liberty and the oppressed love their oppressors. And still he survives and prospers, for yet a little while at least.

---

22. Thomas Hobbes, *Leviathan* (London: Everyman's Library, n.d.), p. 65. Original edition, 1651.

23. George Orwell, *1984* (New York: Harcourt, Brace, and World, 1949).

CHAPTER 2
CAUSES AND
DIRECTIONS

The sense of time and the perception of change are inextricably linked in human experience. The link works both ways; neither time nor change is a dependent variable. One cannot think about change without including the concept of time, and without at least having some sense of its passage. In its simplest form the sense of change really involves perceiving the difference between before and after. "In the old days . . . ," "in the nineteenth century . . . ," "in the Ancient world . . . ," "our prehistoric forebears . . . ," are phrases that introduce all sorts of valid or tendentious comparisons between the wonderful present and the grim past or the glorious past and decadent present. Many such comparisons make time the causal agent of change, cast in the role of hero or villain of the plot. To the pessimist time brings on inexorable decay, a steady deterioration from the largely imaginary, idyllic past. To the optimist time brings on growth and improvement, a steady progress toward the equally imaginary idyllic future. Others see time as a kind of adjunct of change, change that is identified with other causes but is still perceived as a difference between before and after. And if change is viewed as continuous, something more than the mere difference between before and after, the *rate* of transformation may be important. Time, then, becomes the denominator of a fraction, the numerator of which is the number of events that are to be observed or measured.

Without time, then, there is no change. Without change, however, there is no sense of time. At the very least there must be recurrent cycles as a basis for marking off units of time, and the physicist Schlegel[1] has persuasively argued that some change from one cycle to another, some evolution or devolution, is essential for time to be regarded as moving and dynamic and not simply endlessly repetitive.

Time, like space, sets limits on human life and on the variability of social structures. Within those limits time and space are relevant but essentially passive or neutral conditions. They do not *determine* the course of life or the way patterns of social behavior will adapt to or use these "natural" boundaries of social systems. Paradoxically, time has qualities that are essentially static.[2] The division of time into units with finite limits—the hour, day, week, year, the length of the human span of life—sets boundaries and requires the allocation of activties within these boundaries. The tensions that arise from the use of time and from its intrinsic scarcity may well give rise to change, as do other tensions. It is time in its natural form of passage and flow, in its "dynamic" quality, however, that is intrinsic to the very concept of change.

Alterations in the properties of social systems through time thus constitute the focus of social dynamics. In this chapter we shall explore the "qualities" of change, meaning by that concept both the sources and the directions of social transformation. We shall first argue that the qualities vary according to the kind of social organization that we are studying. The order of discussion in subsequent chapters will proceed from the small-scale and short-term to the large-scale and long-term; clarifying and illustrating these distinctions constitute the second order of business for the present chapter. Finally, we shall record and illustrate the principal directions of change, and show how different structures and processes display distinct courses as they move through time.

THE MYTH
OF A SINGULAR THEORY OF CHANGE

The widely voiced complaint, or admission, that "we have no theory of social change" rests on a misapprehension of the nature of social systems and the ubiquity of change within them. Of course, were there some single and invariable "prime mover" that would account for each and every change in the characteristics of patterned action, the social analyst's tasks would be greatly simplified. Any such change could be casually catalogued as another manifestation of the uniform and universal law. The analyst could then turn his attention to other and still

1. See Richard Schlegel, *Time and the Physical World* (East Lansing: Michigan State University Press, 1961), Chap. 1, "Time and Physical Processes."

2. See Wilbert E. Moore, *Man, Time, and Society* (New York: Wiley, 1963).

questionable regularities in social phenomena. This appeal has characterized the various "monistic" theories or varieties of determinism, from biological evolution to the alleged primacy of technological innovation.[3] None of these determinisms has survived the combined onslaught of logical analysis and opposing facts, and the quest was in any event based on false premises and analogies.

One of the analogies wistfully contemplated by social analysts has been the simple and highly general formula for the force of gravity, the "law of falling bodies." This law describes one relationship among masses of matter, and is properly silent on all sorts of other durable or variable qualities of physical objects in various settings. There are, indeed, a host of principles, ranging from the invariant to the probabilistic or statistical, that describe the dynamics of atoms and storm clouds, the speed of light and the evolution of the universe. Although science seeks to relate principles, and to include them in more general and powerful laws, diversity as well as uniformity is a characteristic of nature in all its manifestations.

Since there is no singular theory of social structure in more than a definitional sense, there is no reason to expect a singular theory of change—different types of social organization set different variables for analyzing changes in patterns of action. This sentence says a number of significant things. A social system, as we have already mentioned, minimally consists of role-players or actors in interaction governed by rules of conduct that entail rewards for compliance and penalties for noncompliance. Such systems may vary in size from a pair of friends to the large national state; in duration, from the barely more than transitory encounter to a nominally eternal administrative organization; in range of common interests, from the collector's club to the family or community; and in a multitude of other ways. No simple and universal explanation, such as sociability, will account for this variety, and dealing with variety has been one of the main preoccupations of social science. Descriptive generalizations about particular *types* of systems and explaining the types in their settings constitute the bulk of our very incomplete knowledge of "social systems." A great deal of this knowledge consists of classifications based on one or another range of variation. Although detecting and generalizing the relationships *among* variables is a major goal of science, there is no reason to suppose that all knowledge that would ever excite human interest can be included in one single, simple law.

Changes Related to Particular Structures

The principal basis for organizing our discussion of social change, particularly in the following chapters, will be "structural"—that is, *what*

---

3. A classic critique of monistic theories is that of Pitirim A. Sorokin in his *Contemporary Sociological Theories* (New York: Harper, 1928).

is changing? We have adopted this organization because both the sources and directions of change are partially peculiar to types of social systems. Some examples are in order:

Let us take first an administrative organization, which has an elaborate system of formal rules of conduct that apply in principle to positions and not to persons. One function (consequence) of this system, a function that is probably deliberate and recognized by the leaders of such organizations, is to make the organization relatively impervious to change from the mere fact of personnel turnover. Another feature of such organizations, however, leads to a highly probable sequence of changes that testifies to the importance of persons in a seemingly impersonal system. The way work is done requires relatively small numbers in various organizational units to interact on-a-face-to-face basis. This interaction covers a considerable portion of their waking hours, and, despite personnel turnover, endures from day to day, week to week, and possibly even year to year. These are precisely the necessary and perhaps even sufficient conditions for the formation of "informal groups."[4] Stated in terms of the system, the formation of such informal relationships entails a relaxation of formal rules, a change in behavioral expectations.

This process however, may be traced further. The "actual," as compared with "ideal," norms are likely to be unstable. Here the concept of *perseveration* is useful,[5] which can be crudely translated as carrying things to ridiculous extremes. Relaxation of performance standards or of the strict precedence of authority, an increasing vagueness with regard to the responsibilities of particular positions or persons, the protection of friendly but incompetent colleagues, maintaining a sociable and happy but unproductive unit—these are among the probable consequences of unchecked informality. At some point—one does not say a certain point without more information on particulars—the departure from ideal norms becomes intolerable, probably to higher administrative officers and not impossibly to the consciences of those directly caught up in the situation. Thus a conservative reaction will be instituted. Yet the underlying conditions are favorable to a repetition of the situation, in form if not in exact content; and we are able to observe and predict a recurrent *cycle of sin and penance*.[6]

Even so, the tale is not all told. Were this the end of the matter, this sequence might be regarded as another, although somewhat special, case of the cycle that does not alter the enduring and more general fea-

4. See Wilbert E. Moore, *The Conduct of the Corporation* (New York: Random House, 1962; Chap. 7, "The Unexpected is Ordinary."

5. Ibid., pp. 200, 257.

6. Ibid., pp. 199–201.

tures of the system within which it occurs. The system will be changed, however, particularly in the manner in which rules and sanctions are detailed and specified. No amount of cynicism is likely to dissuade rule-makers from attempting to dampen the extremes to which perseverative tendencies may have gone in the past and to avoid certain manifestations of sin altogether. The cycle, then, is likely to change somewhat as the inventive, ingenious actors pad their parts, while the formal system will change cumulatively as more and more detailed prescriptions for ideal conduct are injected into it.

Any enduring competitive system provides a second example of change growing out of particular characteristics of social structures. Here the significant characteristics of the system are many actors with like rather than common ends, and the ends are themselves scarce. If this situation is to manifest any order at all, it must feature prominently a set of rules that determine the *legitimate* criteria for allocating the scarce values. One possible set of rules, and the one with which we are here concerned, permits individuals or groups to vie for the goals according to a set of rules that limit and specify the means that may be employed. (Unlimited competition is, in a dynamic context, a contradiction in terms, for the means used would be principally force and fraud[7] and both are destructive of the competitive system.) Now this is where the source of change in the system comes in. Outright violation of the regulatory system will be met with sanctions that may be adequate to keep the system relatively unchanged. But "evasive violation," more properly expressed as innovations in competitive strategies, will change not only the relative chances of competitors but may very well destroy the system if permitted to go uncontrolled. Thus innovation will be met by regulation, which either permits the novel strategy under suitable restraint or prohibits its use. In either case we have another principle of social dynamics: *a cumulative regulatory code can be predicted in any competitive system.* We thus reach a destination similar to that reached in our discussion of one kind of change in administrative organizations, but in doing so we traveled a rather different route.

Notice that we have not generalized about the rate of regulatory innovation, nor about the probability that the encompassing system will in fact fail to survive its intrinsically dynamic elements.. This means the prediction of change will take the form, "If the system as stipulated survives, its regulatory structure will exhibit a cumulative addition to the number and associated detail of rules." This is no mean generalization, and although our explanations may have been fairly persuasive, the generalization is not a matter of common sense or something that

7. See Thomas Hobbes, *Leviathan* (London: Everyman's Library, n.d.). Original edition, 1651.

everybody knows. Neither the explanation nor the conclusion is, in fact, common. Yet the fact remains that at this level of generalization, which is abstracted from or overlooks a host of variable details, the possibly critical issue of the survival or collapse of the system cannot be determined. To that question the properly evasive answer is, "It all depends . . . ," and what follows is an indication of some of the more critical differences in administrative or in competitive systems that the process of generalization overlooks.

An administrative organization may in fact lack responsible executives or committed employees who will religiously reaffirm the fundamental goals of the organization and observe its rules. If we had to predict the rate of failure of organizations from internal causes, we should be safest in looking first for instances of rampant conflict between individuals and organized units. But we should also want to mark as likely candidates for demise those organizations whose constituent units seemed to be laughing or enjoying themselves to death. A competitive system may in fact lack wise rule-makers who would scotch an extremely effective and effectively monopolized strategy that would enable the winner to take all, then and forever. That would be the end of the system, not just of the particular contest. One predictive hint here derives from other sociological knowledge. For a competitive system to endure, its participants, or at least the effective makers and enforcers of its rules, must regard the survival of the system as more important than the outcome of particular contests. Failing this criterion, a competitive system is doomed.

The Units for Dynamic Analysis

Clearly, detecting and accounting for common elements among a number of types of structural change is a perfectly permissible inductive procedure. This is the way generalizations are made, if in fact they are made on defensible logical procedures at all. Yet in every process of generalization, losses of particular information have to be weighed against gains in the power of a principle that cuts across otherwise diverse and seemingly chaotic details.

This particular tightrope is no easier to walk than any other, and the conventions adopted here to maintain a semblance of balance should be exposed. For convenience of organization, our "structural" approach to change proceeds from small-scale to large-scale systems. For the sake of technical expression, which is in fact not absolutely required, this may be restated as concentrating first on "microdynamics" and then on "macrodynamics." If we do not limit ourselves in time and place, the rich and populous array of small-scale social structures will require that our treatment of them be far more selective than our treatment of entire societies or the fate of mankind generally. We shall therefore choose those structural types that are most common, without thereby denying that other types may change in other ways. Yet the sources and consequences of change are by no means so affected by the nuances of variation in social groups or social systems that generalization is impossible. We did find that innovations in practices and the consequent additive changes in rules were to be found—for different particular reasons, it is true—in the constrained cooperation of the formal administrative organization and in the competitive system of allocating shared but scarce values.

If we are to adopt a structural approach to change, a small but insistent warning must be reissued, however. Specifying the *unit* to which change is attributed is the first requirement. This precaution is a bit less elementary than it seems, for there may be essential constancy on a large scale despite, or even comprised of, small-scale changes; on the other hand, small-scale structures may appear to persist unchanged while a more encompassing structure is undergoing radical transformation. For example, the socialization of children is a genuine change process for the *person*, but may take place for many persons through generations with no change in the organization of the family, a principal socializing agency. The observation that the family structure has not changed is, of course, tenable only at a fairly high level of generalization, for at lower or more descriptive levels the nuances of interaction between generations and among siblings will in effect change the patterns of action. A governmental agency whose policies and top executives are subject to the winds of political change but is staffed by a permanent civil service, thus maintaining an enduring administrative structure, illustrates small-scale persistence despite large-scale changes. Again, however, in the course of adapting the structure to new policies, some detailed changes in procedures are inevitable.

We may generalize this problem of the unit to which change is attributed. If we take for the moment three aspects of any social system— *actors, forms* (the patterns of interaction) and *functions* (the intended or unintended consequences of action)—each will be characterized by some degree of independent variability. That is, each may change in some degree without substantially affecting the others. And this in turn is a way of reiterating some degree of "looseness" in social systems. This independence is actually least in the small informal or "primary" group, and greatest in large and complex societies. Yet if the conception of social phenomena as a system has any analytic utility and observational reliability, the independent variability among elements cannot be complete or random. If, for example, an administrative organization's main aim is to produce steel profitably and if this aim had no implications for the types of persons hired or for the way they worked together, all our notions of causation, of the relation between means and ends, would be destroyed. Both the selection of employees and their actual behavior would be beyond understanding. If there were no system whereby we could order our observations intellectually, the quest for persistent regularities would be hopeless and change could never be predicted. At the opposite extreme, if any change in personnel or procedures altered the system beyond recognition, then the quest for order would be hopeless at any level of generalization and the quest for orderly change even more so.

In determining why change occurs, two rather general distinctions are useful, and others will appear as we go along. If the element or unit to which change is attributed is clearly identified, it may then be fairly easy to differentiate *internal* and *external* sources or causes. One outstanding advantage of the model of social system with which we are operating is that it permits us to inquire about internal or intrinsic or what Sorokin calls "immanent change"[8] without violating orderly analysis. Of course, in a world that is evil in its complexity, simplifying dichotomies are likely to be plagued by mixed cases and by interaction between internal and external change, but the distinction may still be useful as a starting point. Another distinction, to be used with the same caution, is the one between "accidental" change—often more properly regarded as unplanned, unanticipated, and inevitable, but still explainable —and change deliberately instituted.

Nature rarely provides cases of single and isolated causes followed by single and isolated effects. Usually, causes have causes and effects have effects, which may in turn become causes in the next sequence. Though the search for total understanding is understandable, and indeed prompts the scholar's constant attempts to come ever closer to that goal, in many situations the scientist is fortunate to be able to demonstrate proximate causes for changes, let alone ultimate causes; the *necessary* conditions to predict a sequence of events, let alone precisely *sufficient* conditions. A social scientist who finds this state of affairs unsatisfactory need not think his situation unique. He may contemplate the predicament of the meteorologist, a physical scientist, and perhaps derive some measure of comfort from the fellowship of suffering.

A NOTE ON DETECTION
AND MEASUREMENT

The goal of any scientific field is to advance verifiable propositions concerning the relations among variables. The pursuit of this goal requires first a reliable description or identification of the variables. Often this task involves forming definitions—"We shall identify as passage

8. Pitirim A. Sorokin, *Social and Cultural Dynamics*, (Boston: Porter Sargent, 1957), Chaps. 38 and 39.

rituals those ceremonies that occur on the occasion of a change of social status." So may the definition go. Some methodological purists maintain that scientific definitions must be essentially "operational,"[9] that they must consist essentially of the procedures by which the phenomena are observed or identified or measured. According to this view, the measures determine the units of observation rather than the units determining the measures. Even if we adopt a somewhat less purist view, it is clear that one can make no testable allegations about changes in structures unless there is some procedure by which the structure can be identified and the changes detected.

In many areas of social science, measurement is not very far advanced, so that simple, more-or-less statements can be made but more precise quantities cannot be proved. For example, it may be possible to say from available direct and indirect evidence that crude death rates (deaths per thousand population within a year) were higher a century ago in Western countries than they now are, but not exactly how much higher, or whether the rates were true for all ages or only, say, for infants and children. The refinement of measurement consists of at least two kinds of effort—making the observation and recording of phenomena or events in question more accurate and complete, and developing mathematical and statistical techniques for determining relationships (even partial and indirect ones).

The truly impressive progress made in statistical analysis in recent years has mainly aided cross-sectional and thus essentially correlational analysis. This has fitted the sample survey and similar methods of gathering data. It has also fitted the theoretical orientation to interdependent systems. Thus despite the disputes between socioloigsts with a primarily theoretical concern and those attempting to refine methodology, it can be said with some justice that they deserve one another. Yet certain methodological and theoretical developments are noteworthy. Blau and Duncan[10] have applied a "path analysis" in measuring the factors *and sequence of factors* accounting for differences in occupational mobility between generations, and White[11] has applied a "chain analysis" to the probability of promotion during a career in a bureaucratic organization. Since there is no inherent contradiction between the inter-

---

9. For the concept as developed by a physicist, see Percy W. Bridgman, *The Logic of Modern Physics* (New York: Macmillan, 1949). For use of the concept in social science, an example is provided by Stuart C. Dodd, "Historic Ideals Operationally Defined," *Public Opinion Quarterly*, Fall, 1951, 15: 547–56.

10. Peter Blau and Otis Dudley Duncan, *The American Occupational Structure* (New York: Wiley, 1967).

11. Harrison C. White, *Chains of Opportunity; System Models of Mobility in Organizations* (Cambridge: Harvard University Press, 1970).

dependence implied by the conception of system and a temporal (and thus possibly causal) linkage of components and events, Moore[12] has suggested a "system of sequences." A particular application of a sequential analysis has been applied by Smelser[13] to a step or stage view of various forms of collective behavior. Although Smelser does not attempt quantification of the probabilities of moving from step to step, the theoretical approach would lend itself to measurement.

In a short book, and perhaps in any, discussions of methodology can be as tedious as elaborate distinctions and classifications. Yet a few observations are in order with respect to some special problems involved in detecting and measuring change.

A distinction that is conventionally made in social-scientific writing is one between short-term relations or alterations and long-term ones, although specifying just what temporal periods are covered by each is regrettably uncommon. Thus an economist using an equilibrium model of a market system may point out one or another variety of fluctuation or innovation that disturbs the short-run state of the market but has no long-term effects. Or a sociologist may seek to demonstrate that a change that contributes to the stability or survival of a system in the first instance is disruptive over the long run owing to secondary and tertiary effects—for example, an adaptation in productive techniques for a factory that is to be established in an area lacking experienced personnel and an industrial tradition may serve short-term needs but perhaps may prevent the development of experienced workers who would contribute more to the factory's long-run economic well-being. For the demographer, who deals, among other things, with biological generations, the long-run may be very long. For example, there was a high probability of a "cyclical" decline in the crude birth rate at successive 25–30 year intervals following the low birth rates that prevailed during the Depression of 1930–1935. The reason for this probability on strictly demographic grounds was simply numerical: the smaller number of potential mothers and (less significantly) fathers reaching the ages conventional for marriage and childbearing. This predictable cycle was, incidentally, confirmed in the later 1950's, and early 1960's, thus leading to the expectation of reconfirmation in the 1980's. The "short run" for the demographer—for example, the size and composition of the working-age population 20 years hence, which is almost entirely already living and requires very little hazardous estimating of future birth rates—may look like the "long run" to the economist, who generally deals with shorter time periods. The

12.   See Wilbert E. Moore, "Toward a System of Sequences," in John C. McKinney and Edward A. Tiryakian, *Theoretical Sociology* (New York: Appleton-Century-Crofts, 1970), pp. 155–66.

13.   Neil J. Smelser, *Theory of Collective Behavior* (London: Routledge & Kegan Paul, 1962).

methodological moral here is very simple. Before propositions about short-term and long-term effects can be objectively tested, the time interval must be specified and the future when long-term effects "will" display themselves must not be so distant as to be meaningless. For we are reminded of the acerb comment, attributed to the great economist Lord Keynes, "In the long run we are all dead."

Because it takes so much time to observe change while it is in process, and because of the temporal limits on any investigator's capacity to carry out long-term observations, some changes must either be studied retrospectively on the basis of "historical" evidence, or inferred from "cross-sectional" material. Now historical materials should be as complete and accurate as any scientific data, and if we seek quantities the search may be vain. Because recent data may be more complete and more nearly of the sort that the analyst seeks, or because it may be possible to "manufacture" the data needed by a specially designed investigation, the student of change may seek to "substitute space for time." Suppose that he is concerned with changes in consumer behavior related to rising levels of income, particularly in various undeveloped areas that lack statistics of any sort on consumer budgets or even national statistics on the production and consumption of consumer goods. He finds, however, a classic proposition known as "Engel's Law,"[14] to the effect that proportional expenditures for food are negatively correlated with income levels. This relationship, repeatedly tested and confirmed (though with some differences in exact proportional magnitudes) is based on cross-sectional studies of household budgetary behavior at various income levels. If this difference in "social space" could be translated into a prediction of change through time, one would expect that rising levels of income in developing economies will be accompanied by a reduction in the proportions of consumer expenditures for food. The prediction may in fact be reasonable and at least partially verified by direct evidence as it becomes available,[15] *but it cannot be assumed without direct confirmation.* Kuznets has demonstrated, for example, that the rate of private savings is positively correlated with income at any given time, yet the rate of savings has not increased along with income through time.[16]

Even if we have a continuous statistical record of some social phe-

14. For reference to and discussion of the formulation by Ernst Engel, see Carle C. Zimmerman, *Consumption and Standards of Living* (New York: Van Nostrand, 1936), pp. 29–41.

15. See Richard H. Holton, "Changing Demand and Consumption," in Wilbert E. Moore and Arnold S. Feldman (eds.), *Labor Commitment and Social Change in Developing Areas* (New York: Social Science Research Council, 1960), Chap. 11.

16. Simon Kuznets, *Shares of Upper Income Groups in Income and Savings* (New York: National Bureau of Economic Research, 1953).

nomena, the continuity may in fact be spurious if either the accuracy and completeness of the recording or the identification of the phenomena recorded have changed. An apparent rise in the birth rate or death rate or crime rate may be simply the result of more complete recording of the events. A time-series of consumer expenditures may be partially vitiated by changes in quality or services—for example, retail food expenditures may reflect such changes in quality as the shift from starches and cereals to meats and such changes in processing and in distribution as freezing and pre-packaging. It is not even clear that the current year's automobile is exactly functionally comparable to, say, the 1910 model.

It is caution and not despair that these examples dictate. And the caution rests in part on another paradox: It is the *change* in the qualities of phenomena or in their observation that complicates the problem of analyzing the incidence, rate, or other characteristics of change.

THE DIRECTIONS OF CHANGE

If we accept the position that the question, "What is changing?" is antecedent to all others in making verifiable propositions about social change, the search for a single course or direction of change becomes as dubious an enterprise as the quest for a unique "prime mover." The course of change may be gradual or rapid, peaceful or violent, continuous or spasmodic, orderly or erratic. Thus changes in death rates when civil unrest is rampant may be rapid, violent, spasmodic, and erratic. Long-term changes in the proportion of secondary-school graduates attending college, on the other hand, may be gradual, peaceful, continuous, and orderly.

Though the first of each of these paired alternatives appears related to the others, and the second alternatives seem to be similarly related, they are not in fact simply semantic restatements of a single distinction, as some examples will show.

A "true" revolution, a rapid and fundamental alteration in the institutions or normative codes of a society and of its power distribution, is rapid and discontinuous, by definition, and is likely to be violent, but may well be orderly as opposed to erratic. The short-term changes in stock prices may be rapid and erratic, but peaceful and fundamentally continuous.

Changes in the relative power of employers and labor unions may be gradual, continuous, and orderly but still marked by at least occasional violence. Were the power of unions to increase gradually but without interruption and without limit, the character of the ensuing system of industrial relations would eventually lack continuity with former conditions, for, as Herberg has noted,[17] even the simple doctrine of "more and more" has revolutionary overtones.

Now we must revert to methodology for a moment. The paired alternatives are quite unlikely to be "really" dichotomous, a question of "either-or," but rather may reflect a scale, a question of "more or less." If quantities that measure rate or violence or continuity are developed, then the *interrelation* among these variables becomes a rather useful tool for developing generalizations about the course of change, always with the probability that the generalizations will differ according to the class of changes. One of the interesting possibilities is that the interrelations themselves may be discontinuous. If we examine the relation between personnel turnover and steel production, some turnover is, of course, normal and indeed inevitable in a continuing organization. Within some limits, a higher rate may be positively correlated with higher production, either for essentially extraneous reasons—such as a simultaneous increase in activity in steel markets and labor markets—or possibly for intrinsic reasons if the turnover is accompanied by an improvement in the quality of employees. Yet a very high rate may be mischievous, and the measurement problem becomes one of determining the point at which the relationship reverses or otherwise radically changes.[18]

Despite the wide variety in the possible directions change may take, various generalizations have been set forth. These are worthy of attention, not simply as an exercise in intellectual history, a record of thoughtful errors, but as having some validity if their pretensions to unique generality are suitably downgraded.

Perhaps because there are more optimists than pessimists in the world (or at least among social theorists) or because the lot of mankind generally *has* improved over the long term, by far the most numerous class of theories of the direction of change comprises various *cumulative or evolutionary trends*. Though varying in many ways, as will appear shortly, these theories share a conclusion (or assumption) that by one or another or a combination of criteria of growth, the course of man's history is marked by an "upward" trend through time.

The simplest representation of evolutionary growth is represented by a single straight line (Fig. 1), marking a gradual and continuous development of man's civilization. In a sense this kind of representation is the most generalized of all theories of direction, for it simply abstracts from short-term fluctuations in rates of growth, or the probability that the angle of ascent or even the shape of the curve fitted to various ob-

17. Will Herberg, "American Marxist Political Theory," in Donald Drew Egbert and Stow Persons (eds.), *Socialism and American Life*, (Princeton: Princeton University Press, 1952), I, Chap. 10, especially pp. 491–92.

18. Sorokin has generalized the discontinuous character of any association in magnitudes at some point in degree and time as the "principle of limit." See Sorokin, *Social and Cultural Dynamics*, Chaps. 38 and 39.

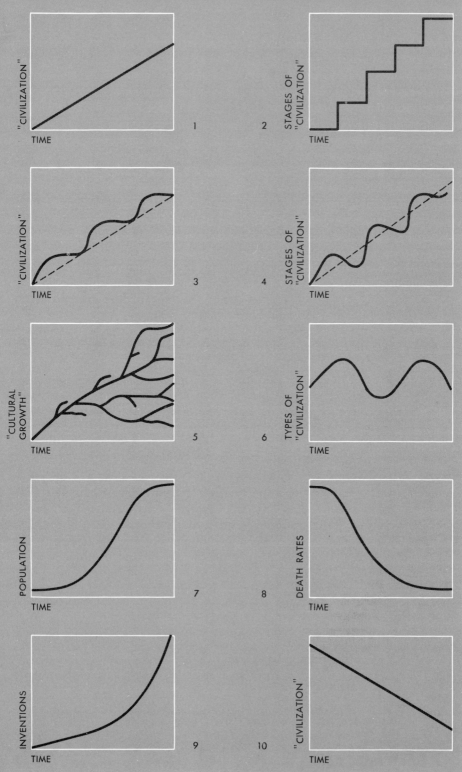

DIAGRAMATIC REPRESENTATION OF THEORIES OF THE DIRECTION OF CHANGE

Figures 1 through 10. 1. Simple "rectilinear" evolution. **2.** Evolution by stages. **3.** Evolution at unequal rates. **4.** Evolution by cycles with short-term reversals. **5.** Branching evolution representing both growth and diversity. **6.** Trendless cycles. **7.** Logistic growth illustrated by population. **8.** "Reverse" logistic growth illustrated by death rates. **9.** Exponential growth illustrated by inventions. **10.** "Primitivism."

servations in successive periods of time would differ as one or another measure of growth is used. Thus it is doubtful that any measure of growth would be precisely rectilinear over the course of human history were information available for plotting numerous points on the chart. *If* all one is after is a crude indication of the *direction* of change between the first available observation or estimate and the last, plus a representation of the *magnitude* of the change only between the beginning and the end, then a straight line connecting the two points will illustrate these two kinds of information. One would hesitate, however, to use such a generalization as a basis for predicting the future, for the actual course of change may have been more nearly like the "logistic" or "exponential" growth curves we shall discuss presently. (Figs. 7 and 9). Yet even the straight-line representation of the direction of change may be approximately accurate over shorter periods and for particular types of social phenomena. For example, the *average* increase in productivity (output per man-hour of work) over an entire economy such as the United States may be fairly regular and gradual over considerable periods of time.[19] Even here, however, the angle of ascent would be different for various sectors of the economy, and for various periods, and the single line would represent a substantial "loss of information" through generalization.

Concern for marked unevenness and even discontinuities in rates of growth has given rise to various "stage" or "cyclical" theories of growth (Figs. 2, 3, and 4), of which the "stair-step" notion (Fig. 2), is again the simplest. Such stage theories were at one time very popular with theorists of "social evolution," as we saw in Chapter 1. They are, however, far from dead either in the thinking of laymen or in the writings of scholars. Ancient history books and the early chapters of world history books subscribe completely to the idea of successive (and progressive) eras of man's civilization, marked off by relatively sharp breaks between one era and another. One mode of classification attends primarily, at least for early stages, to

19. See John W. Kendrick, *Productivity Trends: Capital and Labor*, National Bureau of Economic Research. Occasional Paper No. 53. (Princeton: Princeton University Press, 1956).

the materials used for tools and weapons: the "Old Stone (Paleolithic) Age," the "New Stone (Neolithic) Age," the "Bronze Age," and the "Iron Age." Another mode of distinguishing stages, not always neatly integrated with the first, concerns itself primarily with the dominant mode of economic production: hunting and food-gathering, pastoral nomadism, settled agriculture, industry. Intermediate and specialized or localized stages may also be identified—for example, the burning-clearing-shifting cultivation in tropical areas as intermediate between nomadism and settled agriculture. And the quest for order that proceeds by identifying distinct stages does not end with the ancient or historic past. The present and recent past have been characterized by a variety of partially overlapping and partially competing "ages": steam, steel, electricity, automation, nuclear energy, outer space.

If accurate observations could be recorded and plotted at close temporal intervals, it is unlikely that anything as formalized as the precipitous alterations in tools or technology represented in Fig. 2 would result. Yet over the long term, and in ignorance of the precise rate at which innovations such as fire, or metallurgy, or the domestication of animals were in fact adopted, the undoubted inaccuracy of the representation may be tolerable.

In most examples of "stage" theories the discontinuities are caused by changes in man's relation to his environment—that is, in technology. Yet the same underlying notions could be, and occasionally have been, applied to quite non-material changes: for example, in the discontinuous transition from primitive animism to sophisticated monotheism in religion and theology. Auguste Comte argued that man's intelletual evolution could be represented as consisting of three stages: theological, metaphysical, and "positivist" (or scientific).[20]

A somewhat less severe and stylized representation of growth at uneven rates yields a theory of developmental cycles with a long-term "upward" trend (Fig. 3). Again this type of theory has been popular in historical scholarship, particularly with respect to the history of the Western World. In Fig. 3 the first peak might be represented by Greco-Roman civilization, the second by the Renaissance, and the third by the Industrial Revolution. Such sweeping views are likely to be more useful as literary devices than as scientific representations of change. Yet again, this depiction of the course of social phenomena may be appropriate on a smaller scale. One example of inequality in rates of change that may have rather wide applicability is the sequences of *innovation* and *accommodation*. The increase in size of administrative organizations, as measured by number of employees, may look very much like Fig. 3 over a period of

---

20.   Auguste Comte, *Cours de Philosophie Positive* (Paris: Rouen, 1830–1842).

years or decades, the increases perhaps stemming from new product lines in a manufacturing concern and the stable periods representing consolidation of the new activity within the organization.

Some theories of long-term changes concede that matters may retrogress temporarily, though reaching higher peaks (and indeed higher troughs) in ensuing cycles. Figure 4 resembles conventional representations of business cycles in capitalist economies, with cycles of prosperity and depression repeating earlier cycles (although not exactly), as the economy shows an underlying trend of steady growth, say as measured by gross product or income per capita. One may derive a faint bit of wry amusement by applying the same theory of change to the Marxist theory of history. As this is a "dialectic" theory of change arising from conflict between classes as representatives of inconsistent interests, the top of any cycle might represent the "thesis," the bottom the "antithesis," and the transitory periods when the society is on the intermediate trend line the "synthesis." Of course for Marxist theory, the curve could not be extrapolated endlessly, for at the point of post-revolutionary synthesis, when the classless and stateless society is achieved, structural change would cease and the "civilzation" line would presumably be high but certainly horizontal.

Uneasiness over the level of generalization reflected by many cumulative or evolutionary theories has led some scholars to attempt to combine unity and diversity within the single conception of "branching evolution" (Fig. 5). Though a single line fitted to the points represented in Fig. 5 would show an upward course, it would fail to indicate that some cultures or civilizations show a relatively unchanging or even downward movement; and lines not reaching the right-hand boundary represent cultures that have not survived to the present. Although a diagram representing real data would require some single measure or combined index of measures concerning what constitutes growth for the vertical axis of the chart, something like the conception of branching evolution may provide one form of valid generalization of man's history. At almost the opposite extreme of generality, branching evolution could be applied to the progressive specialization of occupations involved in making a single product. By comparison with the craftsman who carries the production from raw material to finished product, the division of labor may entail employment of workers at higher and lower skill levels, and the creation of some occupations that soon cease to be needed at all.

The "logistic" curve of growth represented in Fig. 7 appears to have been first applied to social phenomena with respect to population growth. Raymond Pearl,[21] pursuing an analogy between the growth of cells in a

---

21. Raymond Pearl, *The Biology of Population Growth* (New York: Knopf, 1925).

laboratory with an initially hospitable but clearly finite environment, reasoned that human populations might behave in a similar fashion over a long period and on a grand scale. Although the assumption of constancy in the human environment is demonstrably invalid, the representation may be approximately accurate in places that are initially sparsely populated and over periods not marked by abrupt changes in man's command of the environment. Hornell Hart has applied the conception of the logistic curve to a wide variety of phenomena,[22] while taking into account the effect of changes in important conditions which may curtail a particular trend or start a new one. Figure 8 represents a "reverse logistic" with respect to the downward course of mortality, which may fall very rapidly with gross improvements in food supplies and sanitation, then much more slowly as one approaches the "ideal" state of affairs in which no one dies except of old age. Since a decrease in mortality rates is depicted by a descending line, and since this is a trifle unsettling after a steady reign of left-to-right progress, the trend represented in Fig. 8 could be made more palatable by recording the course of average expectation of life at birth with falling mortality, the curve once more resembling the one in Fig. 7.

The "exponential" (or compound interest) rate of growth takes into account the steadily expanding base on which growth rates are calculated. Although this kind of growth curve (see Fig. 9) has been associated primarily with inventions or technological changes (the argument being that the more principles to be combined, the more novel combinations are to be expected,[23] although approximately at a steady rate), it actually has much wider application. Since children, when they mature, are likely to have children of their own, unrestricted population growth may resemble the diagram in Fig. 9. (Indeed, notice the similarity between Fig. 7 and 9. An observed exponential rate of growth may be simply the middle sector of a logistic curve, preceded and followed by slower growth rates.) On a broader scale—indeed, the broadest, comparable to various long-term evolutionary theories—it can be reasonably argued that if the vertical scale is to represent not inventions but the combined rate of all changes in large-scale social systems, then the rate of such changes is accelerating, and the steep upward slope of the curve may understate the rapidity of contemporary change and the prospects for future change.

Most of the cumulative or evolutionary theories of social change can

---

22. Hornell Hart, "Social Theory and Social Change," in Llewellyn Gross, *Symposium on Sociological Theory* (Evanston, Ill.: Row, Peterson, 1959), Chap. 7. Hart also presents diagrammatic representation of other forms of social change in this paper.

23. See William F. Ogburn, *Social Change* (New York: Huebsch, 1922).

be illustrated by the kinds of growth curves represented by the simplified diagrams we have just been discussing. And in an eclectic and tolerant sort of way we have accepted them all, if not at their original values, then at bargain prices to explain small-scale and short-term changes in human behavior. We have not disposed of evolutionary changes yet, however. Just as the conception of branching evolution has sought to preserve the idea of a general trend without submerging the apparent diversity of societies and their courses of change, other evolutionary conceptions have sought to encompass the relations among the various components of change, which may not always follow one another in an invariant and convenient temporal order. One form of evolutionary change, called *cumulative retroactive evolution*,[24] though difficult to present diagramatically, has been illustrated in the context of economic growth and social change:

> An example of this evolutionary pattern may be found in the sequence of development between the commodity market and factory employment. Because of the culture of the hypothetical society in the preindustrial phase, commitment [acceptance of the norms in a system of action] starts in the market. Once a market has at least started and developed to some extent, commitment can start in factory employment, in that the nature of commitment in the market was such as to remove the previous cultural blocks to wage labor. However, full commitment in the market in turn may depend on the development of a high level of commitment to factory work. [Money turns out to have increasing uses.] Thus the sequence between the two loci (contexts of action) reverses itself and is "retroactive." The theory is not a determination of "prime movers" and rectilinear sequences, nor simply a functional correlation, but a sequence with alternating directions. . . . An analogous pattern of change operates in economic systems, as where an initial agricultural revolution makes possible a diversion of productive factors to manufacturing, which in turn makes possible agricultural mechanization, chemical fertilizers, and rapid delivery of agricultural products.[25]

These illustrations demonstrate the complexity that attends particular structures and processes of change, which make the general theories we have been discussing both impressive in their generality and inhibiting in their inattention to otherwise important characteristics of social phenomena. The conception of "cumulative retroactive evolution" could not have arisen either from a simplifying theory of rectilinear change from a single primary and everlasting cause, nor, clearly, from a theory of self-equilibrating systems. It is the combination of *order* in systems

24. See Arnold S. Feldman and Wilbert E. Moore, "Moot Points in the Theory," in Moore and Feldman (eds.) *Labor Commitment and Social Change in Developing Areas*, pp. 365–66.

25. Ibid., p. 366. Quoted by permission of Social Science Research Council, publishers.

and *changes* in that order that is important for dealing with the dynamics of shorter-term and smaller-scale theories than with grand theories of man's fate, yet not at the level of trivial or transitory detail.

There is a particular form of representing the direction of change that is also evolutionary in the sense that the transformation is cumulative and directional. This is the *theory of economic development and social change,* which involves analyzing the processes associated with industrialization or economic modernization. In the study of these processes, which has grown rapidly since World War II, several interesting conceptualizations have emerged. Most of the studies have used what amounts to a "transition model." That is, industrialization (to use a shorthand term for the complex of changes) is seen as once-to-a-system transformation, repeatable in space through time. Time figures as an explicit variable in two and possibly three ways: (1) as delimiting the period during which the society or economy is in transition; (2) as a basis for comparing the speed of one transition and another—for example, the probability that contemporary industrialization may be faster than earlier experience, partly because a broader spectrum of experience is available and need not be precisely duplicated in either sequence or timing; (3) less frequently, time figures as a basis for determining the rate at which the pattern spreads from one system to another.

One particular aspect of modernization is sometimes called the "demographic revolution":

> The broad empirical generalization is that pre-modern populations were comparatively stable. High and relatively constant fertility rates were offset by high and variable mortality rates. With modernization, death rates were reduced; and fertility rates were reduced considerably later, with the result that there was rapid transitional growth. The transition is presumably completed when low and relatively constant mortality is matched by low and variable fertility.[26]

This transition model may be represented by two reverse logistic curves, with a time gap between them, as depicted in Fig. 11. Again, if progress consists of moving upward, the curves could be consolidated and inverted, with the vertical scale indicating something like the efficiency with which pre-modern and modern populations reproduce themselves.

Although students of economic development readily concede that the changes accompanying modernization are complex and not necessarily uniformly sequential, a rather simplified transition model is often implied in scholarly writings. As Feldman and Moore have commented critically:

---

26. Wilbert E. Moore, "Industrialization and Social Change," in Bert F. Hoselitz and Wilbert E. Moore (eds.), *Industrialization and Society* (Paris: UNESCO-Mouton, 1963). Chapter 15, p. 327.

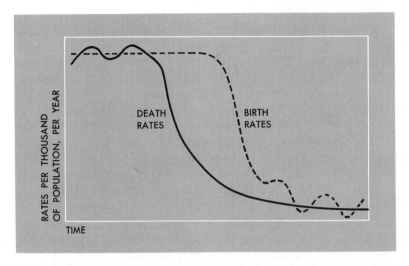

Figure 11. The "demographic revolution" occasioned by economic and social modernization.

Economic transformation is viewed as the intermediate phase of a three-stage model of social transformation: (a) a static, pre-industrial stage, (b) a dynamic, transitional stage, and (c) a static stage following the industrial revolution.[27]

This kind of a change model, represented in Fig. 12, is clearly wrong in exaggerating the static qualities of pre-modern societies, and grossly wrong in implying that rapid change ends with the completion of the transition to industrialism. By a variety of separate measures or a combination of them, change in industrialized societies more nearly resembles the exponential curve (Fig. 9).

Despite the great interest social scientists have shown in the intermediate transitional stage of the three-stage model of economic development and social change, a great deal more is known of before-and-after comparisons than about the sequence and rate of changes. Although the propositions derived from these studies are by no means inconsequential they do leave unanswered significant questions that are concealed by any single-line representation of the direction of change.

We cannot yet descend from the high plane of general theory, however, for we must attend to certain less comforting conceptions of change. One world-weary generalization, which essentially argues that all man's

27. Arnold S. Feldman and Wilbert E. Moore, Industrialization and Industrialism: Convergence and Differentiation," in *Transactions of the Fifth World Congress of Sociology,* Washington (September, 1962), 2:152.

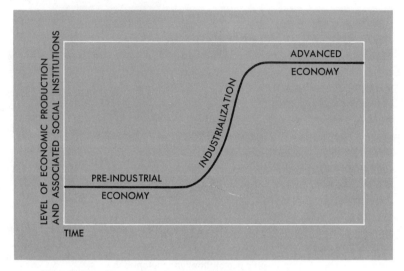

Figure 12. Common but unacceptable "transition" model of industrialization.

experience has happened before—a kind of sense of *déjà vu* on the grand scale, the disturbing sensation that we have been along this way before—does not deny change, but does deny that it is leading anywhere over the long term. Oswald Spengler's theory of the life cycle of civilizations[28] may be represented as a trendless cycle (Fig. 6), and Sorokin's theory of the alternation of Ideational, Idealistic, and Sensate cultures[29] takes a similar form, although Sorokin would attribute considerable stability to his middle type—a somewhat stable mixture of faith, reason, and senses as the source of truth (Fig. 13).

Before leaving the subject of trendless cycles, it is appropriate to remark that for a variety of social phenomena, changes may be essentially cyclical if rates only and not underlying quantities are recorded and plotted on a graph. For example, the short-term course of marriage rates and birth rates in contemporary western societies essentially goes up and down without an evident trend. A trend would be introduced by plotting the number of married persons or the size of population. Similarly, if one diagrams innovation and accommodation, not as illustrated in Fig. 3 with an underlying growth trend, but simply as alternating emphases in some aspects of social systems, a trendless cycle might once more appear.

Although we need not take seriously the position of extreme his-

28. Oswald Spengler, *The Decline of the West* (New York: Knopf, 1932).

29. Sorokin, *Social and Cultural Dynamics*.

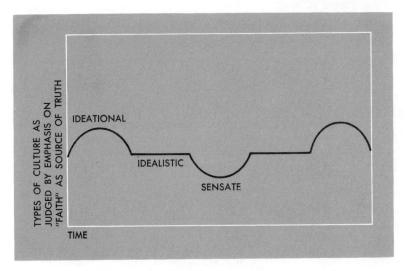

Figure 13. Sorokin's three types of culture, diagramatically represented as a trendless cycle.

torical relativism, which essentially maintains that there are *no* general trends of consequence, it should be remembered that not all changes are necessarily directional in any significant sense, or perhaps even consequential for the social analyst. And here once more we must add a methodological note. First, the form and direction of change clearly are in part a function of the time periods and observational units. Second, the shape of a curve fitted to trend data accordingly depends in part on the detail demanded—for example, a curvilinear trend may be made rectilinear by greater generalization (and consequent loss of information or "goodness of fit"). Third, wherever reliable quantities are available, the mathematical alternatives in curve-fitting are much more numerous than the simplified models presented here. Fourth, the possible formal models are further multiplied if "interaction in process" or other complicating features are introduced.

Any theory of the direction of change may be associated with notions of progress, which is not a scientific concept but a value judgment—change in an approved direction.[30] Thus many of the variants of evolutionary theory assume that growth, say in levels of living, or size of social units, or man's command over his environment, are progressive, and indeed would be were the changes welcomed with universal acclaim, which is extremely unlikely. Even cyclical theories may be interpreted in terms

30.   See R. M. MacIver and Charles H. Page, *Society* (New York: Rinehart, 1949), Chap. 28, "Social Evolution and Social Progress," especially pp. 610–15.

of progressive change, especially where there is an underlying trend toward long-term change, and short-term progress is also not barred. When Fig. 4 is used to represent economic fluctuations, for example, the long-term trend of growth is viewed as progressive; but over the short term, progress consists of getting back to the trend by dampening and reversing the extremes of inflation and deflation. A similar idealization of the middle course or middle phase in trendless cycles (Figs. 6 and 13), is also common.

One interesting and persistent evaluation of social trends is very common in the social theories entertained by laymen, and by no means unknown among scholars. This notion is expressed in the concept of "primitivism,"[31] which in its simplest form may be expressed as the pessimistic view that mankind generally or any particular social system is retrogressing from some former and better state (Fig. 10). The idealization of the happy "state of nature" or the "noble savage" is one variety of primitivism, but others are more restricted. Among historians and critics of national literatures, the concept of a past "Golden Age" is a common convention. In fact, nostalgic distortion of the past is a favorite gambit of the critic of things current. The nineteenth century is often depicted by American critics as a time of individualism and freedom, of rural virtue and pioneering spirit, of democratic social life and easy mobility between generations and within careers. That there is little or no evidence for these idyllic views of the past does not utterly destroy their social significance as manifestations of discontent with the present, but does serve to warn the social analyst that he is dealing with a curiously inverted evaluation of change by which progress consists of "going backward," a reconstruction of a lost (and largely mythical) past.

With regard to theories of the direction of change, leaving aside the evaluation of change in terms of progress or decay, it is possible, as we have seen, to view many or most of them not as competing generalizations but as appropriate to different aspects of social systems. For the most part, the models we have examined entail plotting the intersection of only two variables—some quantity (or rate or index of growth) and time. More complex analytic models, which would permit several or many treacherous variables to be handled simultaneously, may be developed by methodologists. For the moment, partial theories appear to be the best that can be expected, whether in terms of the sources of changes or the directions of their course through time.

---

31. See H. O. Lovejoy, *et al., Primitivism and Related Ideas in Antiquity* (Baltimore: Johns Hopkins University Press, 1935).

CHAPTER 3
SMALL-SCALE
CHANGE

Change is so much the natural order of human existence and social life that it comes to be taken for granted, to excite no curiosity or surprise. This is particularly true of standardized sequences. Changes in behavior from minute to minute or year to year appear normal and regular, either because a person, the actor, has played this part before and knows his lines and stage directions, or because others have been this way before.

A child's first day in school, for example, marks a transition that has been traditionally endowed with high emotion, almost trauma, if not for the child then at least for his mother. The child is beginning a new phase in his life, in the order of his time, and in his behavior, and the mother's predominant position in her child's life begins steadily to erode.

Nursery schools and kindergartens may blur the formerly sharp transition from the pre-school world to a formal system of disciplined instruction, just as moving from adolescence to adulthood may be clearcut or prolonged and attenuated. The blurring complicates the appraisal of the transition from infancy to childhood, but does not alter the fact that there is a transition.

But is this social change? It is certainly individual change in the life pattern of the child. And the downward extension of the school, or at least supervised play, marks a change in the "educational structure" and therefore in the functioning of the family. But whether a child's progression through the educational system, or any person's movement through a succession of positions and roles, exemplifies *social* change is not so easy to answer. In principle it does not, so long as the process is accompanied by no *significant changes in the group*—that is, by no alterations in the positions and their relations and thus in the performances people are expected to play, in rules of conduct, or the results of the system as it continues to operate. The question becomes partly one of fact. What and how much effect do individuals have on the group or organization or pattern of action? This is the first question. The second is: What and how much effect constitutes social change? The second question is more difficult to answer, for it involves a decision concerning the purpose of the analysis. At what level and for what periods does one seek to generalize and predict? If one is interested in the nuances of patterned behavior among children and between teachers and pupils, very "fine" observation will be necessary and a "change model" must be used for analysis and generalization that will pick up regularities in the alterations in patterns. Otherwise the adaptation of the structure to the individual may be so minor and idiosyncratic that it defies any meaningful generalization, except the essentially negative one that enduring structures with changing personnel must be marked by some "flexibility," and that its precise patterns will exhibit "fluctuations."[1]

Since our approach to social change is primarily structural, an analysis that requires a prior stipulation about what is alleged to be changing, the rich variety of social groups and organizations, and of recurrent patterns of action is slightly embarrassing. "Small-scale changes" may be so small, and so peculiar to particular structures, that a catalogue of such changes would be virtually interminable, and even the most curious seeker after tiny bits of social information would sooner or later find himself bored to the teeth with the whole enterprise. And properly so. Unless in fact we can achieve some level of generality, some way to knowledge from one situation to another, the endless variety of "microdynamics" would defeat all sense of intellectual order.

Fortunately our predicament is not so precarious. At worst we can deal with types of groups and small-scale systems, and not with unique structures; and although the number of different types might also be pushed rather high, we are under no complusion to be so particular.

By small-scale changes we shall mean changes in the characteristics of social structures that, though comprised within the general system identifiable as a society, do not have any immediate and major consequences for the generalized structure (society) as such. The line, of course, is not absolutely sharp, and may be somewhat arbitrary. The qualifier "major" is possibly evasive, unless some measure of magnitude is available and

---

1. Sorokin has emphasized the importance of "fluctuations" as essential in directionless change in a variety of contexts of action. See, for example, Pitirim A. Sorokin, *Society, Culture, and Personality* (New York: Harper, 1947), especially Parts Six and Seven.

some meaningful "critical minimum" is accepted as constituting a major effect. Then, too, time perspectives enter to plague us, for small-scale changes may have no major consequences for society over the "short term" but persistent and directional changes in any structure within a society are almost certain to have significant general effects eventually or over the "long term." If there were no such linkages, the conception of an entire society as a social system would have extremely weak factual foundations. If the linkages were close and complete, we should be once more in the dilemma that any small-scale change would be either trivial or tragic, as we discussed in the first chapter. Anthropologists and sociologists are generally most impressive when they trace out the connections between, say, a given change and a consequence in some seemingly remote aspect of culture or social action. Yet surely the examples are a radically unrepresentative selection from among the myriads of variations and changes that are essentially inconsequential.

What we are seeking are changes that although essentially inconsequential insofar as alterations in the structure of society are concerned, are nevertheless orderly and predictable and not mere meaningless meandering.

The small-scale changes that permit a considerable measure of generalization may be initially classified into four broad categories: (1) repetitive cycles of social action, (2) changes in the structure of groups, (3) the dynamics of inter-group relations, and (4) the consequences of inconsistency in values and rules of conduct. The variables that might be used for one or another type of structure—size, duration, mode of recruiting members, breadth of their common interests and rhythm of activities, for example[2]—then become either relevant conditions for particular types of change, or, in some cases, dynamic variables.

SOCIAL ACTION IN CYCLES

All enduring groups or social patterns exhibit characterstic rhythms. Even in those rare instances where a small group of persons is in "constant" interaction (or constant for the waking hours), the rhythms required for bodily functions, the ordering of the various collective activities in some sequence, impose a cyclical pattern of recurrence. Some of these cycles may be most appropriately viewed in terms of "social time"—that is, the cycle as such defines the time interval.[3] However,

2. Ibid., Chaps. 21–28.

3. Ibid., pp. 682–85. Chapter 45 as a whole, on "Direction, Rhythm, Periodicity, and Tempo in Sociocultural Change," is relevant here.

some attention to at least crude astronomical time will be evident also—daily, monthly, or annual cycles. Though the "week" has no astronomical base (any more than the hour, minute, or second), such periods intermediate between the day and the month are also very common.[4] These weekly cycles include "rest" days as well as religious observances, feasts, or fasts, and periodic marketing days. Daily, monthly, seasonal and annual cycles abound and even longer periods—for example, the scholar's nominally seventh sabbatical year away from normal teaching duties.

Short-Term Cycles

Change of pace, resulting not only from physiologically necessary sleep but also from periodic changes in the pattern of activities, appears universally in human societies. Some of these changes of pace are clearly tied to man's environmental relations—the celebration of the annual food harvest, for example, or even the temporally irregular but still patterned participation in a successful hunt or booty-collecting raid. These alterations in the "normal" routine, and especially those alterations that have a fairly fixed and therefore predictable temporal order, appear to serve as tension-releasing mechanims. Some of them, and particularly those that merely afford periodic respite from normal demands, provide primarily individual tension-release, although they are not thereby socially negligible. Some festivals clearly serve "integrative" functions by symbolizing communal or collective values and allegiances. The phenomenon of the patterned "moral holiday," the temporary waiving of conventional restraints and taboos, provides *controlled deviance* and probably thereby reduces nonconformity. Many cultures indeed provide periodic, usually annual occasions for changes in the normal structure of power and prestige and in the deference and respect accorded to constituted authority and even sacred objects and persons. Slaves became masters for a day in many periods in classical Greek and Roman history; peasants might play at being lords once a year in Medieval Europe; in contemporary Latin-American countries a nominal religious holiday may be turned into comic portrayals of secular rulers and sacred personages.

These relatively short-term cycles still contribute change if a sufficiently short time period is used as a basis of observation. Over the longer term, their recurrence marks an element of order, and their results may precisely prevent more disorderly or changeful manifestations of the normal tensions intrinsic to patterned behavior.

We now encounter an association of variables that is by no means

---

4. See Hutton Webster, *Rest Days* (New York. Macmillan, 1916).

complete. Small-scale cycles and indeed most small-scale changes tend to be short-term ones, and with the exception of life cycles, long-term cycles tend to be large scale. Since revolutions are large-scale and short-term (at least as measured by their conspicuous manifestations) the relationship is not reversible. In fact if we adopt a conventional two-by-two or fourfold classification (see Fig. 14), it is only the small-scale but long-term change that is doubtful, again excluding life-cycle phenomena and excluding also the possibly cumulative (and therefore scale-increasing) long-term consequences of persistent short-term changes.

The apparent absence of small-scale but long-term *cyclical* change may correspond to the real situation in social systems, but we cannot be absolutely confident of that. Short-term cycles, although relatively inconsequential for changes in society as a whole, tend to be readily detected by laymen and scholars alike. Relatively inconsequential long-term cycles, and particularly those that leave no strongly visible evidence, as would be true of cycles in clothing fashions or in art styles, are likely to go unrecorded and unobserved.

Life Cycles and the Family

The human life cycle of course represents a relatively long-term change in individuals, in which we are not primarily interested. What is of interest is the way that man's biosocial nature—his birth, infancy, maturity, and mortality—affects the patterns of action in the systems of

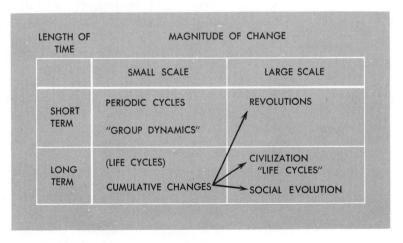

Figure 14. Representation of relation between magnitude and temporal dimensions of change.

which he is a member, and in particular imposes a cyclical pattern on the family as the social structure responsible for the biological recruitment of new members, early sustenance and socialization of infants, their initial extra-familial social placement, and for some continuing intergenerational relations after children have matured and formed "new families."

This cyclical pattern, though durably repetitive, is not without uncertainties and strains. We discussed in Chapter 1 some intrinsic sources of variability in the processes whereby infants are "incorporated" into the structure of the family and other structured components of societies: individual biological differences interact with differences in birth order, differences in the structural position and particular variations in the internal interaction of family members, differences in the actual as compared with ideal composition of kinship systems, variations in the personality and interaction patterns of age peers outside the family, and so on. Under these circumstances anything like a precise duplication of role performances and relationships in continuing structures is highly unlikely. Yet this information indicates only that fluctuations in social action certainly will occur and that possibly, but with a probability that could be determined only by specific information—the structure as specified simply fails to persist. Otherwise, fluctuations in structures owing to uncertainties in socialization, and consequently essential variations in role demands, do not appear to yield propositions that would enable us to predict consistent directions of change.

Yet on further thought, these short-term variations may indeed have long-term cumulative consequences. The key insight for this line of speculation is the possibility of structural failure (or radical alteration in patterns and consequences) owing to intolerable extremes in role performance. Because success and failure are unlikely to be dichotomous, but rather characterized by various scales of approximation to ideal performance at one extreme and deviant performance at the other, *any enduring structure will exhibit an accumulative body of rules*, relating at least to defining limits on one or another aspect of actions appropriate to positions. We have encountered this principle before with respect to competitive systems and administrative organizations, and now by a still different route it appears as a proposition of impressive generality.

Any structure that makes age-specific demands on persons experiences a turnover of age (or birth) cohorts. The graded school is an outstanding example, but at least some minimal succession of persons in age-relevant patterns of action and therefore some succession of patterns of action by individuals moving through age categories are universal features of human societies. And even if the membership criteria or specific role expectations in organizations are not highly limited or specified by age, an enduring organization still faces the inexorable fact of man's mortality and thus, once more, the variability that arises from the changes of "players" in particular roles.

Although true "generational" cycles may occcasionally occur in organizations other than the family—as when an organization is entirely comprised of age peers and keeps its membership intact until the first death, which may be fairly shortly followed by others until the entire membership is changed over a few years—they are relatively rare. It is in the family that the individual life cycle has the most general and significant consequences.

The three critical events affecting most families, whether the family is viewed as a two-generational or multi-generational structure, are marriage, birth, and death. This is the order of the events if we look at the primary or "nuclear" family. The family is formed by a marriage, which, in view of the "incest taboo," will prove a link of some sort between different lineages. That link may be strengthened by the birth of children, as the lineages become related through the succession. Since many societies, however, have socially recognized one line of descent, and therefore kinship, to the exclusion of the other—matrilineal or patrilineal— it is only in "multilineal" systems such as our own that marriage and birth provide a linkage between descent groups.

The principal point of present interest is that marriage is always strain-producing, possibly for the marital partners, but certainly for the kinship system as an enduring structure, for marriage entails the incorporation of a "stranger" into one or another descent group, or possibly into both.

Birth also is strain-producing, at least in terms of the problems of sustenance and socialization that infants pose. And death, particularly of one spouse, disrupts if it does not fracture the family unit. For the continuing kinship system, death presents problems of succession—for example, to hereditary positions or to control of property. It is not mere coincidence that these events—birth, marriage, and death—are marked by *passage rituals*, which function both as "informational" activities concerning a change of membership and status and facilitate the emotional conditioning appropriate to an altered set of role requirements.

There is one other aspect of the succession of generations that requires comment. The length of a biological generation in the human species is not fixed, and indeed has a rather wide potential variability. The potential reproductive span of women extends from puberty to menopause, that is from about age 12 to age 45. Now variations in the actual interval between ages of parents and children have both a small-scale and a potential large-scale significance. The exact patterns of interaction between parents and children are likely to be affected by age differences. And if there are "external" changes in such components of social systems as general standards of conduct, the degree of intergenerational conflict is likely to be correlated with the age span between the generations.[5] Similarly the age of parents when mothers cease childbearing will, along with the life expectancies, determine the probable duration of primary families as two-generational units before the married couple possible reverts to an effectively childless state—the quaintly phrased "stage of the empty nest."

The *average* length of generational cycles will affect the rate of population change except in the unlikely situation of births canceling out deaths. A reduction in the age of marriage and childbearing, for example, will increase the rate of population growth even without increasing the number of children per family, simply because there will be less delay in the speed with which children become parents. The Taeubers have calculated that during the American "baby boom" of 1945–1954, younger brides and earlier childbearing together accounted for 64 per cent of the increased number of births compared with the 1930–1939 period. Another 24 per cent stemmed from former population growth, reflected in an increase in the number of women of child-bearing age; and only 12 per cent represented an increase in family size.[6] We have here then another example of the small-scale change, representing largely optional and separate decisions of young people before and after marriage, which had both large-scale and long-term consequences.

CHANGES IN GROUP STRUCTURE

In patterned or structured or organized social action, the effect of individual personality is mediated through "role performance." Now the effects of role performance and of interpersonal interaction on group structure are variable but never nil or zero. The relevant factors that determine or correlate the magnitude of individual imprint on the group merit examination.

Using conventional sociological teminology, we may distinguish the "primary" group—the small, face-to-face, and enduring aggregates characterized by many common interests and by emotional intensity of interaction—and the "formal association"—the large, internally specialized organization, with one or a very few common interests and highly specific impersonal interaction.

From our definition of the primary group, we may expect that changes in the nuances of the relationships *and therefore* in structure

---

5. See Kingsley Davis, "The Sociology of Parent-Youth Conflict," *American Sociological Review*, August, 1940, 5:523–35.

6. Conrad Taeuber and Irene B. Traeuber, *The Changing Population of the United States* (New York: Wiley, 1956), pp. 267–68.

may be virtually continuous. In the formal association, on the contrary, prescribed relationships apply to offices and are antecedent and subsequent to particular incumbents. In this type of structure the change wrought by mere individuals should be small and relatively intermittent or rare.

These and similar types of social systems, though useful for some purposes of social analysis, actually represent "syndromes" of component variables, and those variables may in fact not vary in perfect correlation. Since pure types rarely if ever exist "in nature," departures from purity in one respect have an uncertain significance for predicting change of any other aspect of the organizational type. In sum, it is often preferable to treat the structural variables singly or in small combinations rather than in global "types."

The Individual and the Group

Our aim is still to detect how a person individually and in association with others will affect the structure of groups.[7] By taking several variables singly, we may predict that this individual influence will be *positively* correlated with:

the range of interest or functions attributable to the group
the degree of affectivity socially expected
homogeneity or similarity of "expected" role performance
the extent of democratic participation in decision-making and particularly the occasions for unanimity

No doubt other correlates could be added, but verification of these and others depends on clear-cut procedures for identifying and measuring variables. The same strictures apply to the variables that are predicted to be *negatively* correlated with individual impact on organizations:

membership size
rigidity and specificity of nominal role requirements
specialization of positions and roles
"authoritarian" decisions

Here we encounter a possible interruption in the seemingly neat relationships, the break involving the range of homogeneity and specialization. Where homogeneous performance is the norm, the individual with variant capacities or even interests may effectively change the norm

---

7. See Wilbert E. Moore, "Social Structure and Behavior," in Gardner Lindzey and Elliott Aronson (eds.), *The Handbook of Social Psychology*, 2nd ed. (Reading, Mass.: Addison-Wesley, 1969), Vol. 4, Chap. 32, pp. 283–322.

at least in minor degree. An attempted or prospective major change is likely to produce a crisis and possibly punishment or exclusion for the deviant. Where specialization is highly developed, the specialized individual may have very limited minor effect; but the interdependence of specialized activities means that the effect may also be major—disruption of the system by extreme deviance or failure in performance. We thus conclude that the influence of individuals on complex organizations (to revert to the use of a constellation of variables as a type) is more likely to be negative than positive from the standpoint of the organizations' continuity or effectiveness in fulfilling collective interests.

We should, however, mention once more the danger of dealing with types, particularly if they are identified with concrete organizations rather than treated as analytic ideas. Although a person may have little or only a potentially disruptive effect on the *formal* structure of complex organizations, virtually every concrete example of such organizations of the important sub-type, the bureaucracy or administrative organization, will display evidence of changes growing out of individual interaction. The situation is relatively simple. Such organizations provide the necessary conditions for the formation of "informal" groups.[8] These groups may serve or hinder the mission of the official organization that provides the conditions for their existence, or may in fact be irrelevant. But any influence at all is very likely to induce change in the formal structure, in its rules and procedures and in role requirements, in order to combat negative influences and to incorporate positive ones. Thus the individual and his "informal" interaction patterns may in fact be a source of change in structures where the individual seemingly counts for little.

Even the single individual may affect massive organizations, because it is virtually impossible, in a structure that must withstand turnover, to insure exact duplication of performance in positions. Where employee recruitment is carried out with strict regard to merit and without regard to prior social relationships, there will be some measure of organizational adaptation to convert the stranger into the member. This prediction arises from a realistic insight rather than from the formal model of the organizational type. The insight is to the effect that the individual, however highly qualified, will not know all the precedents and procedures that have been developed in the particular organization. Though the adaptation of the neophyte to the organization is the change that normally comes to mind, the point here is that some adaptation of the organization, some time and energy by organizational representatives, must be devoted to introducing and "socializing" the newcomer.

8. See Wilbert E. Moore, *The Conduct of the Corporation* (New York: Random House, 1962), Chap. 7, "The Unexpected Is Ordinary."

"Group Dynamics"

The most extensive observational studies of the interplay of individuals and groups have involved "small" groups—with "small" often not defined but rarely embracing more than 20 members and usually less than 10.[9] Many, and perhaps most, of these observational or experimental studies are identified by their authors or others as dealing with "group dynamics."[10] The problems set for the various investigations mainly consist of (1) changes in individual behavior (or even personality) in a multi-individual situation that may or may not qualify as a "group"; or (2) actual changes in the role patterns played by individuals and in group rules and results. Now individual changes are not our primary concern here, and generalizations about group changes are remarkably few relative to the volume of studies that have been carried out. These generalizations at times deal with functional relationships but do not explain the *sources* of change.

In sum, it is not unfair to say that most of the work on "group dynamics" neither concerns groups as small-scale social systems nor changes in the significant dimensions of those systems. This curious situation arises because the large majority of scholars in this field are psychologists, for whom the individual is the significant element to be studied; and whether the observations are conducted by psychologists or sociologists, the great majority of studies have involved experimental groups rather than those in natural settings, and thus the principal sources of change have been in fact the experimenters, and hence have been external to the system under analysis.

Let us examine some of the nominally "dynamic" (but actually functional) relations in small groups. For example, *size* (the magnitude and changes in which are not explained) is correlated with:

role specialization and the formation of internal coalitions

indirect communication, and particularly the proportion of all communications addressed to leaders

increase in the total real or potential number of relations; if direction of relationship is distinguished, the number of interpersonal relations is $n (n - 1)$, where n is the number of persons; if the "bond" or relation is the unit, then the potential number is $\dfrac{n (n - 1)}{2}$

9. Olmsted, in his extremely useful summary of this subject, set the limits at two to twenty members. See Michael S. Olmsted, *The Small Group* (New York: Random House, 1959), pp. 22–23.

10. See the papers assembled by Dorwin Cartwright and Alvin Zander (eds.), *Group Dynamics* (Evanston: Row, Peterson 1953)

Some other propositions depend on typologies or at least distinctions of types. For example, a spontaneously formed group is likely to exhibit a high level of positive affect (friendliness) among members. Again this is not a very "dynamic phenomenon." Nor are such relations as that between specificity of group function and the degree of internal role and status differentiation, including formal leadership statuses or the likelihood that rationality will be emphasized in selecting procedures. The requirement of unanimity within the group, a requirement that may be the result of hostile external pressure, is likely to result in:

1. an increased volume of communication, particularly in messages to the minority
2. techniques of consent: compromise, appeal to higher principles, or even ejection of the minority

Occasionally, however, real dynamics appear. Where groups have a task-orientation as a kind of externally imposed condition for group action and affective (warmly personal) interaction as an internal condition, leadership relating to the two functions may be differentiated and competitive, and a kind of "dynamics of vacillation" appear.[11] Bales and Strodtbeck say that a task-oriented group will move through distinct phases—orientation, evaluation, and control—and that as these phases develop, member reactions, both positive and negative, will increase.[12]

Bales also argues[13] that role structures (and thus norms) grow out of the need for predictability. This view thus becomes a partial theory of group *formation*, but in the context of Bales' work it appears that a group, or at least an experimental aggregate of individuals, is already at hand. Sorokin[14] remarks that the ultimate reason for group formation is the inadequacy of the isolated individual, but the ways in which groups originate may be *spontaneous:* the chance encounter and discovery of common and complementary values and interests; *deliberate:* the selection of members in terms of particular goals to be achieved; or *coercive:* the imposition of membership by superior power or authority. Although examples of any of these processes of group formation come readily to mind, no particularly systematic study has been devoted to the conditions under which one or another process is likely to occur.

---

11. See Robert F. Bales, *Interaction Process Analysis* (Cambridge: Addison-Wesley, 1950), pp. 153–57.

12. Robert F. Bales and Fred L. Strodtbeck, "Phases in Group Problem Solving," in Cartwright and Zander (eds.), *Group Dynamics*, Chap. 26.

13. Bales, *Interaction Process Analysis*, pp. 15–16.

14. Sorokin, *Society, Culture, and Personality*, Chap. 21, "How Groups Originate and Become Organized."

Groups also may break up or "die." Here Sorokin[15] has suggested certain conditions or correlates of group survival, most of which are "optimum points" or ranges between extremes: size, homogeneity and heterogeneity of members, rigidity and elasticity of structure, openness or restrictiveness of membership, equality and inequality of position, and so on. These constitute suggestions for possible measurement rather than predictive propositions as they stand. Sorokin does generalize that speed in group formation is negatively correlated with "longevity," and (again "within an optimum point") that size is positively correlated with group persistence.[16]

Changes in Formal Organizations

Although bureaucracies or administrative organizations appear to be about opposite in type to the small group, we have already mentioned that the individual may have an impact leading to change even there.

The bureaucracy, however, shares with other social systems various sources of internal strain, of which the relation of the individual to the group is only one. Competition, for example, serves primarily in these complex organizations to determine merit. This competition prevails among individual aspirants for preference and promotion, but also among administrative units and divisions.[17] And competition, as we saw in Chapter 2, produces an accumulation of rules of the game, a trend in change shared by other enduring systems but for different particular reasons.

Administrative organizations provide ample opportunities for conflict as well as orderly competition. In the ideal state of such structures the several goals of the organization are exactly ordered in priority, the means to those goals are clear and unchallenged, the resources of the organization are distributed in ways that receive uniform consent, the power of officers is exercised with justice and the willing consent of subordinates, jurisdictions are never in dispute, advisers and administrators complement one another perfectly, and the structure maintains a "united front" in its dealings with external interests and pressures. This ideal state includes major specifications of a common "model" of administrative organizations, but each item in the list actually constitutes a source or site of strain and possible change.

15. Ibid., Chap. 34, "Life-Span, Mortality, and Resurrection of Groups."

16. Ibid., pp. 532–33.

17. See Moore, *The Conduct of the Corporation*, Chap. 8, "Competition." With respect to the whole discussion here of change within administrative organizations, see also Chap. 9, "Conflict," Chap. 13, "Two-Faced Experts," Chap. 14, "Evolution, Revolution, Reaction," and Chap. 15, "Innovation and Inhibition."

Disputes over both goals and means are likely. Goals are generally stated rather abstractly but must be specified before they become the ends of action; and, perhaps more importantly, permanent organizations tend to add functions as they grow and the precise priority of functions is more ideal than actual. The occasion for setting such priorities may arise only in adverse situations when scarce resources make it impossible for the organization to achieve all its goals simultaneously. The means for achieving goals are subject to dispute because of ignorance and un-certainty, and therefore some lack of predictability or basis of choice among alternative proposals.

The probability of real disputes and not simply inconsistencies arising rests on another organizational characteristic—that the various alternatives have genuine spokesmen whose specialized positions, their duties, require them to pursue one or another line of endeavor. If the corporate treasurer or financial vice-president emphasizes profits and re-lations with stockholders, the community-relations man "votes his con-stituency" on behalf of the company's community responsibilities, the personnel man speaks for the "development of the human potential" of employees, the marketing vice-president speaks for consumer interests. Where ends are not an issue, the various routes to the destination may still be. In order to expand the sale of products, better design, cheaper production, and increased advertising will each have its advocates.

If we grant that strain and conflict are to be found in administrative organizations, that the legitimacy of graded authority is subject to chal-lenge, that control of operations or resources provokes contests, that there is a whole array of distinctions between line and staff officials, what has this to do with change? The simplest answer is that these departures from perfect harmony constitute problems, and in an organization where ra-tionality is institutionalized—that is, made a general norm of conduct and decision—problems provoke attempted solutions. Individuals seek to fur-ther their interests, or, very commonly, the interests of organizational units they represent, and in doing so attempt to find new strategies of competition and conflict, to create new procedures, new distributions of power, influence, prestige, and wealth.

The divisive influences, however, need not dominate. Some problem-solving will be directed toward alleviating tension or removing strains, and will lead to compromise or to authoritative and disciplined decision. Neither perfection in such attempted solutions nor cynical acceptance of departures from the ideal model should be expected.

There is another possible source of change from within administra-tive organization that might be termed "deliberate problem-creation." Particularly but not uniquely in industrial corporations, change itself has become organized and institutionalized. Persons, and indeed whole units, such as research and development departments, are assigned the task of deliberately inventing or improving products, processes, organizational principles, or forms of public relations. Although many of these changes may be directed nominally toward altering the organization's external environment or its adaptation to it, any innovation in fact adopted has further organizational consequences. These include new functions and opportunities for disputes about goals, means, and jurisdictions. Since the innovator is, organizationally speaking, a "troublemaker" and is normally a staff expert and not a line administrator, the deliberately innovated change intersects with many or most of the other endemic strains we have already discussed.

The pattern or direction of probable change in bureaucratic organization is mixed. Some trends, such as the cycle of sin and penance, are likely to be repetitive, again with an underlying accretion of regulations. Others, such as various fashions and fads in organization and procedure, may be short and essentially inconsequential, although again some accretion is likely if we consider the broad category of imitative changes and not particular ones. One additional source of change, although it provides only moderately firm bases for forecasting trends, is also deliberate. This is the widespread, though largely non-rational, doctrine that an organization must grow or die.

> This is clearly one of the strongest forces for continuous change in the contemporary corporation. It affects participants at nearly every level and in nearly every functional position. Each year should be better than the last, and the phrase "bigger and better" tends to be redundant, because bigger equals better.[18]

Since in many organizations (particularly those that do not measure success in terms of money) the principal index of success may be growth, the doctrine may be self-confirming, although still subject to doubt insofar as the relation between growth and the real goals of the unit or the system as a whole is concerned. Size carries penalties not only of possible maladjustment to the environment and possible collapse but also, internally, of disproportionate increases in the "overhead costs" of communication and administration. Despite these strictures, enduring organizations *are* likely to grow over considerable periods, and with precisely predictable consequences in their internal structures.

The key to change in another type of organized system, the voluntary association, is to be found in the designation "voluntary." The implication of this restraint on the organization's control over the individual is that the association must compete with others for the individual's scarce

18.   Ibid., p. 196.

resources, including his interests or loyalty and his time.[19] Associational membership is thrice discretionary: the potential participant may choose whether to join any association, and, if so, which one, and within the organization what his level of participation will be. If the association's "time inventories"—the number of member-hours devoted to its activities —are used as an index of participation—its direction of change, will be as follows:

> The most probable historic course of the person-time assets of associations would be represented by a relatively short but steep initial rise in the "time-inventory curve," reflecting a combination of growing membership and initial high participation on the part of each, followed by a gradual decrease as member hours if not actual members are reduced. A new function, a new "service" to members, or even a new urgency in the goal in a proper "interest group" may temporarily reverse the trend, followed inevitably by a new decline. In some cases, such as the political party or club, recurrent elections may provide the environmental occasion for political revivals. A sustained high pitch of participation is quite unlikely, however, and any attempt to achieve it is likely to require exceptional inputs of time in order to provide a "never-ending" supply of novel appeals.[20]

This "standard" course of associations is represented in Fig. 15. On inspection, it is remarkably similar to the course of life expectancy at given

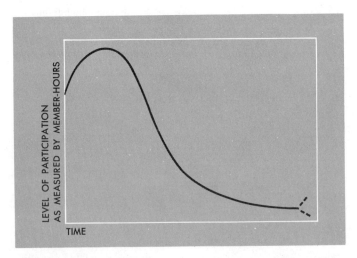

Figure 15. Representation of the course of participation in associations.

19. See Wilbert E. Moore, *Man, Time and Society* (New York: Wiley, 1963), Chap. 6, "Voluntary Associations."

20. Ibid., pp. 163–64.

ages in relatively underdeveloped areas, where infants that have survived the first brief interval after birth have a *higher* expectancy of continuing survival than newborn babies, but thereafter share with all members of their species the risks of death, which will sooner or later overtake them. As social rather than biological systems are involved in the case of associations, we should not push the analogy with organisms to the ultimate. Associations may in fact achieve a measure of durability not only longer than the lives of their members, but also beyond the association's success or failure in its original mission, for one of the hidden but important characteristics of organized groups is the "quest for immortality." If this quest is successful, it is more likely to reflect the satisfactory state of personal interactions than the orientation to tasks. The relation of these two functions or consequences of social groups is so uncertain that successful groups in terms of achievement of tasks may have been quite unsatisfactory in terms of individual aspirations for expression or value of personal relations. Combinations that have been quite successful at achieving collective goals may persist because of their beneficial side-effects. The interesting cases are in effect those organizations that survive success, for they have defeated the normally effective principle of "attrition of interest," usually by inventing new goals and claims on interests.

A special feature of nominally voluntary and democratic associations is worth mentioning. Power is usually a reward for participation, which tends to be highly differential:

> The active participant need not seek power. It will be thrust on him, in the guise of "responsibility." Time may be money in the economic marketplace, but in the voluntary association time is power.[21]

Increasing the participation of members adds to the store of scarce resources, including time and loyalty, but may threaten the distribution of power. Thus any voluntary association is faced with a dilemma. It must either slowly decline into a totally ineffectual organization, both in its announced mission and in the individual "psychic" rewards it can provide for participants, or it must suffer the probability of structural change as a consequence of renewed dedication to the enterprise.

Since associations as such do not make decisions, which are in effect made by officers and other members in some mixture of official and personal capacities, the abstract or organizational formulation of this dilemma should not be taken too seriously. The probable course of associations through time is the one that we have noted: a decline toward demise. The penalties of refurbishment, of establishing a new level of participation, are likely to be too heavy to be undertaken. This is not an "iron law" like the structural law of the domination of associations

21. Ibid., p. 165.

by minorities,[22] for in fact hardy believers do occasionally persist, and even more occasionally do succeed in reviving associations and sufficiently altering their bases of appeal to achieve a nice combination of persistence and novelty.[23] Such associations, and they are understandably rare, follow a course of change that resembles a cycle comprised of a succession of "reverse logistic" curves such as the one illustrated in Fig. 15. It would not be unduly cynical to predict that cycles after the first will start at successively lower levels. This postpones the final demise, and alters its course, but does not finally evade it.

Both administrative organizations and associations exemplify another source of unequal power, that deriving from the differential distribution of relevant knowledge. This knowledge may consist of the law and lore of the organization, permitting the possessors (who are likely to be "sound organizational types") to withstand conscientious but technically improper challenges. It may even consist of strategies of organization and "cooperation": the application, for example, of some of the conclusions from "group dynamics" about styles of leadership and the encouragement—within guarded limits—of participation as a device for capturing loyalty.

The manipulative use of differential knowledge, though perhaps relatively durable where the knowledge is in effect highly technical, as in the case of the learned professions, is not likely to have the same lasting efficacy where there is a substantial latitude in permissible learning and where alternative sources of information are available. In these more open situations, and they are rather common, no manipulative strategy can survive its recognition as such. Thus we encounter another dynamic principle, that *techniques of manipulation will have a very short useful life,* and a consistent policy of using superior but not very esoteric knowledge for controlling others will require a high rate of inventive activity in concocting new devices.

The association's competition for members' time exemplifies a more general source of change deriving from the relations among groups with overlapping membership. Multiple memberships, or at least multiple role requirements, are a ubiquitous feature of the human condition. It seems highly improbable that these present themselves to actors with neat congruence, since universal scarcities restrain social participation and the fulfillment of all role demands. With a bit of playful alliteration we may

---

22. On the "iron law of oligarchy," applied by its author to political parties, see Robert Michels, *Political Parties*, trans. by Eden Paul and Adar Paul (Glencoe, Ill.: Free Press, 1949). See also the analysis of Michels' work in Neil J. Smelser, *Sociological Theory: A Contemporary View* (New York: General Learning Press. 1971), pp. 50–58.

23. See Sorokin, *Society, Culture, and Personality*, Chap. 34.

identify these scarcities as *time, treasure* (or material resources) and *troth* (loyalty or affective energy). These three scarcities are often interrelated, so that allocations of loyalty may be indicated by allocation of time or treasure or both. However, they are analytically distinct. Any viable social system requires norms that determine allocation of these scarcities, but the latter remain omnipresent sources of strain in individual behavior and in the relations between and among various groups and social categories.

Thus groups, or, more properly, representatives of groups fulfilling role demands, are likely to vie for the scarce human resources that they must somehow share. This competition in turn provides the minimum behavioral basis of role conflict, which we thus perceive to be a pervasive strain in social existence, and not simply the product of some abnormal conditions of inconsistency in values and norms.

That this competition for members will produce at least minor changes in particular group structures is readily apparent. The form and degree of such change is, however, impossible to specify in general terms. Yet in the character of relations *among* groups with overlapping membership we encounter another source of accumulation of norms. The question of equity is always relevant to any particular allocation of scarce resources, and the equity of any system of differential allocation of scarce values is subject to challenge as to both principles and results. The challenge may not be constant and consequential but rather intermittent, as when a new role demand is made without a corresponding reduction in existing ones. The changes in action patterns in situations of crisis or disaster represent extreme examples of changing role demands,[24] but the argument here is that we do not have to search for abnormal and external sources for the opposing tendencies: normative regulation of collective claims and the probable persistence of strains that have not been prevented or resolved by existing principles of allocation. What we are saying in effect is that these small-scale changes arising from competing claims on common members with scarce resources have larger consequences for the system of which they are a part, including especially the probable growth of "customary law" as unforeseen strains and conflicts are somehow resolved through additions or amendments to "principles."

Even in societies that value "pluralism" and thus accord to groups and organizations a considerable autonomy in internal rule-making and other elements of structured action, the autonomy cannot be complete if for no other reason than the incomplete and often tenuous claims on constitutents.

---

24. See Neil J. Smelser, *Essays in Sociological Explanation* (Englewood Cliffs, N.J.: Prentice-Hall, 1968), Chap. 8, "Toward a General Theory of Social Change," especially pp. 221–32.

RELATIONS
AMONG PRECLUSIVE GROUPS

Some types of concrete structures have preclusive memberships within a broader social system. That is, membership in one organization or category within a particular class virtually precludes membership in others in the same class. One normally joins only one religious denomination, political party, or occupational association, and is likely to recognize common interests in only one ethnic or "racial" category or, possibly, a "social class." In non-literate societies mutually exclusive lineages hold a prominent place in the social landscape, and they are rarely inconsequential anywhere.

As a crude approximation, the relations among preclusive groups may be said to be insulated, complementary, competitive, or conflictful. Though "complete" isolation of a group is rare, as this would mean that the group was "in the society but not of it," approximations may be found in the sectarian religious community or the radical and illegal political group. Yet effective insulation may mark the relations between other social categories: ethnic groups that have no direct contact, families that remain ignorant of one another's existence or in any event share no common social affiliations and activities.

In all situations other than effective insulation, the relations between mutually exclusive groups are strain-inducing and thus probably change-producing. This is clearly true of competitive and conflict groups, but even those that are apparently complementary are likely in fact to display elements of competition and conflict. The most obvious case perhaps is to be found in the relations between managerial and "labor" groups, which, though complementary in function, compete or struggle over the distribution of power and income. In many instances the seeming distinction between complementary functions in fact leaves the exact jurisdictions uncertain and subject to rivalry: physicians and nurses, lawyers and tax accountants, clergymen and psychiatrists, teachers and parents.

In some instances a distinction so simple as "we" and "others," or the in-group and out-group, may be approximately accurate. This is especially true in conflict situations, which tend to become inexorably two-sided rather than many-sided; and neutrals are likely to be viewed with intolerance by contenders: "If you are not for us you are against us." Yet such a dichotomous distinction will be a distortion of many situations, where a "social distance scale" is likely to be more appropriate. That is, "others" are likely to be regarded as near to or distant from one's own position or values and not lumped together indiscriminately as "outsiders."

Differences among groups and categories are often represented or signaled by *status* and *situs symbols*. The former refers to symbols of position where a fairly clear scale of preference of higher and lower applies. The great popular interest in status symbols,[25] an interest apparently shared by many sociological scholars, has tended to distract attention from the multitude of symbols of membership that have no readily identifiable "scalar" value, or at least not one on which there is any substantial consensus. These give rise to situs symbols. Rotarians may feel superior to Lions Club members, but the latter will not agree that Rotarians are, and third parties are likely to be indifferent. The same is likely to be true of religious or political affiliation, which may have local rankings difficult to generalize from one place to another.

Our interest in these symbols of affiliation is that they may be "used" in a sense both offensively and defensively. They are meant to identify and exclude, but like all interaction strategies they are likely to have very transitory utility. *The degradation of status symbols is a universal dynamic principle,* the only questions being rate and route of diffusion. New symbols are likely to be created at a rate somewhat proportional to the decay rate. Situs symbols are subject to the same fate whenever they take on the taint of invidious distinction.

For the relations between competitive or hostile groups, studies of ethnic relations provide one of the richest stores of "process" propositions. The codification of principles by Robin Williams[26] provides a valuable summary of the results of many studies. Williams states hypotheses or propositions, with explicit assumptions and conditions, dealing particularly with intergroup tensions and their reduction. He deals with the origins and prevalence of hostility and with types of hostility and conflict, and then proceeds to the section of most interest to us, the factors in the incidence of hostility and conflict. Some of the principal generalizations follow.[27]

THE MINIMUM CONDITIONS for intergroup conflict are *visibility, contact,* and *competition*.

DIFFERENCES in *values* enhance the probability of conflict, which may then exaggerate the differences that led to the "categorization" or "stereotyping" of visible group differences in the first place.

THE PROBABILITY OF INTERGROUP conflict is also related to: increases in the

---

25.   See, for example, Vance Packard, *The Status Seekers* (New York: McKay, 1959)

26.   Robin M. Williams, Jr., *The Reduction of Intergroup Tensions*, Social Science Research Council, Bulletin 57 (New York: 1947)

27.   This summary is based on *The Reduction of Intergroup Tensions* by Robin Williams. Ibid., pp. 54–60.

number and differentiation of groups; rapid social change (even if favorable, such as increasing prosperity); the prevalence of tensions and forms of social "disorganization"; a high level of relatively unfocused aggression deriving from decreased predictability in interpersonal relations.

THE PROBABILITY OF MASS CONFLICT, however, is *reduced* by multiple minor cleavages and a number of vulnerable minorities.

Mass violence (e.g. race riots) is most likely under the following conditions: (a) prolonged frustration leading to a high tension level; (b) presence of population elements with a propensity to violence (especially lower class, adolescent males in socially disorganized areas); (c) a highly visible and rapid change in intergroup relations; (d) a precipitating incident of intergroup conflict.[28]

Although conflict itself represents a variety of social change, it is likely to have other consequences. Groups in conflict are likely to increase their internal "cohesion" by long-standing sociological principle. And as between the groups, not only are innovative strategies, counter-strategies, and the control of strategies in the "public" interest to be expected but so also are efforts to achieve compromises or to alleviate the surface tensions or their underlying causes.

Where preclusive groups are in a situation of constrained interaction, such as management and labor, or "loyal" political parties, their interaction will result in mutual modifications in internal structures. Thus collective bargaining between management and unions results in the probable addition in both camps of specialized bargaining staffs and possibly research staffs dealing with issues in disputes. If labor policies are set on a company-wide or industry-wide basis, the power of national union officers will increase relative to the officers and members of local union groups. Although some strategies may destroy the relationship—the "loyal opposition" ceases to be loyal and seeks illegal means of gaining power, the union's demands drive the employer out of business or the employer's policies undermine the union—an enduring relationship will, once more, be marked by accumulative rules and precedents. Following these rules and precedents will in turn steadily reduce the "independence" of the separate contenders, for they are in fact partly united by their jointly developed rules covering the relationship.

NORMATIVE INCONSISTENCY

Even with apparent consistency among the components of a "normative system"—the aggregate of rules of conduct—groups and systems with

28.   Ibid., p. 60.

overlapping memberships make inconsistent role demands on individuals. Yet normative consistency itself cannot be assumed. Some change-producing elements of inconsistency in standards of correct behavior will conclude our survey of small-scale changes.

The literature of sociology abounds with divisions of social phenomena into two sharply separated categories—for example, traditional and modern, primary and secondary, *consanguine* families emphasizing common descent and *conjugal* families emphasizing the marital union, social cohesion based on homogeneity and cohesion based on interdependent specialization. Although such modes of classification are "primitive" in the sense that they attempt analysis in terms of attributes rather than variables, they are not useless. It is the beginning of wisdom to identify the dichotomies as polar extremes on a range of variation, and the pursuit of wisdom to observe that pure types do not concretely exist. A very considerable gain in wisdom results, however, from recognizing the paired alternatives as conflicting principles of social organization and regulation, both of which are persistent in groups and societies. Emphasis on one alternative in the values and norms of any society or group does not dispel or dismiss its counterpart.[29]

A few illustrations of this essentially *dialectical* view of social systems may serve to indicate its possible value in resolving some theoretical diffculties that stem from the customary notions that assume stable "integration." Sociologists have noted, for example, that assignment of position and rank on bases over which the individual has no control, such as lineage or sex or birth order, does not entirely evade questions of competence or merit. Put in technical language, *status ascription* is intermixed with *status achievement*. Societies such as our own that emphasize achievement always retain elements of ascription. It is also to be doubted that predominant attention to common descent as the strongest familial band entirely dispels the probable emotional bonds arising in the *conjugal* relation, and conversely. By this view the persistence in contemporary American life of various reciprocities among adult brothers and sisters and between adult generations is not anachronistic, a mere survival of an older kinship system. Despite the functional connection between conjugal families and industrial societies, and despite inequalities in the social mobility and positions of the separate family units, substantial kinship linkages can be observed, and there is no basis for predicting their disappearance.

What we are suggesting is that such distinctions as ascription-achieve-

---

29. This view has been developed independently, but without primary application to social change, by Reinhard Bendix and Bennett Berger in "Images of Society and Problems of Concept Formation in Sociology," in Llewellyn Gross (ed.), *Symposium on Sociology Theory* (Evanston: Row, Petersen, 1959), Chap. 3.

ment or consanguine-conjugal, although usually depicted as mutually exclusive alternatives useful for characterizing differences between societies or groups, are more accurately viewed as conflicting principles always present.[30] When Sorokin discusses alternative forms of social relationship (familistic, contractual, compulsory[31]) or forms of government (authoritarian, democratic[32]) he describes them as forms that "fluctuate" in their predominance through time. It appears more useful and more consistent with the data to account for such "fluctuations" by the continued presence of competing principles.

Though a strictly dialectic view of contending opposites helps to "make sense" of a long array of dichotomous distinctions, and has a certain appeal from intellectual history, this may be yet another example of the simplification that we seek to impose on phenomena to give them an understandable order. As implied in Sorokin's three-fold alternatives noted in the preceding paragraph, there may be more than two contending principles.

This view of the normative order does not yield a prediction concerning the direction of change except as "fluctuations," or possibly cyclical sequences, having one or another predominant principle. At the very least, however, it does introduce a conception of intrinsic strain and a propensity to change.

These and other sources of "immanent" change—we have noted a number in this and previous chapters—have been criticized by Catton as "animistic" rather than the "naturalistic" theories that he prefers.[33] Naturalistic theories, in his view, are observationally based, and we have consistently stressed the observational basis for intrinsic sources of social change. Therefore Catton's objections can be dismissed as tendentious. On the other hand, Smelser[34] has accepted the view of intrinsic tensions and strains in society, and suggests that the problem of indeterminacy of direction may be alleviated by attention to the "political

---

30. The same comments apply to the paired alternative normative principles that Parsons calls "Pattern Variables." See Talcott Parsons, *The Social System* (Glencoe, Ill.: Free Press, 1951), esp. pp. 188 ff.; see also Parsons, "Pattern Variables Revisited: A Response to Robert Dubin," *American Sociological Review*, August, 1960, 25:467–83.

31. Sorokin, *Society, Culture, and Personality*, Chaps. 5 and 29. See also Sorokin, *Social and Cultural Dynamics*, one-vol. ed. (Boston: Porter Sargent, 1957), Chaps. 38–39.

32. Sorokin, *Society, Culture, and Personality*, Chap. 30.

33. William R. Catton, Jr., *From Animistic to Naturalistic Sociology* (New York: McGraw-Hill, 1966), especially pp. 14–17, 118–19.

34. Smelser, *Essays in Sociological Explanation*, especially pp. 260–80.

apparatus" of societies and thus ". . . the posture and behavior of the integrative and mobilizing forces."[35] This is quite consistent with the emphasis elsewhere in this exposition on deliberate change, and with our characterization of society as a *tension-management* system.

Persistent strains also figure between ideal and actual norms, which we remarked about in a general way in Chapter 1. These have clear implications for intra-group relations. Thus "practical" norms are likely to exhibit perseverative tendencies, to depart farther and farther from the ideal, a trend recurrently interrupted by conservative reactions. Moreover, since rules fit general or type cases, the process of adjudication of particular cases is also and necessarily a process of accumulative legislation. The notion of a perfectly comprehensive code of rules suitable for every occasion is a fiction, and, like other "integration" or "equilibrium" models of social systems, has been more useful for understanding the persistent order in a social system than in predicting modifications in that order. Such a fiction is perpetuated, for example, by Merton's famous "paradigm" relating to forms of deviance.[36] Innovation, identified by Merton as a type of deviant behavior, in which culturally prescribed goals are pursued by illicit means, may also be "evasive" when no rules relate to the novel tactic. This leads to the probability that either practices or principles change, and possibly both.

Finally, the institutionalization of rationality means, inferentially, the institutionalization of change—for the problem-solving orientation seeks "the better way." Yet all enduring groups and organizations accumulate precedents and establish traditions. Until challenged, "the way it has always been done" is the right way, and no degree of emphasis on rationality is likely to prevent conflict between tradition and its upholders and rational innovation and its partisans. It is a commentary on the degree that change in modern societies is not only expected in a cognitive sense, but also encouraged in a normative sense, that spokesmen for time-honored procedures are likely to be characterized by the derogatory term "vested interests."

In any event, change may produce tensions as well as remove or alleviate them. Although many of these tensions and changes are indeed small-scale, they are not trivial or incapable of more general understanding and prediction.

35. Ibid., p. 280.

36. Robert K. Merton, "Social Structure and Anomie," in his *Social Theory and Social Structure*, rev. ed. (Glencoe, Ill.: Free Press, 1957), Chap. 4.

CHAPTER 4
CHANGES IN
SOCIETIES

As we begin the discussion of social change in tribes or nations, or, as sociologists prefer to call encompassing social systems, *societies*, we encounter a domain prominently occupied by historians. For though there are special histories of art or science or literature, a great deal of scholarly history is devoted precisely to "cultures" or "civilizations" and particularly to their political organization and military fortunes. We need have no feeling that the historians' occupation of these territories is preemptive. Our only necessary caution is that our interpretation not do grave violence to the kinds of descriptions and sequences that comprise historical learning, while necessarily eschewing the nuances and details that enrich historical writing.

Historians on the whole have a "vested interest" in the uniqueness of situations and events, and analytical social scientists are prejudiced in favor of the generalizable elements in otherwise diverse data. Neither position is categorically right or wrong, for the purposes of scholarship are rather different. Yet exaggerating the diversity may obscure the efficiency of generalization where appropriate, and overemphasizing common elements may blur the fact that differences are significant.

The historians' emphasis on the *particular* antecedent factors contributing to an event may be quite justified as long as the event is to be explained in terms of its unique qualities. Yet even here choice must be made among the limitless number of antecedent circumstances, and that choice is likely to rest on some sense of causal efficacy, some priority in the probabilities of influence. In other words, if historical *intepretation* is attempted, as distinct from "simple" but endless and meaningless recording of situations and events, then at least an implicit theory of change is almost certain to be involved. Antecedents and consequences rarely are simple and isolated, and an interpretation of their connections must rely on a measure of generality, of comparative experience, to be persuasive.

Much of our discussion here will be rather far removed from the peculiarities of history, but not so far removed that historical application would be impossible. For although we cannot meet the challenge of history, if by that we mean accounting for unique events, we must attempt to *identify recurrent combinations of antecedents and consequences*. To the degree that identification is possible, we shall be able to generalize and to predict, and thus abandon the comfortable situation in which events may be made to appear inevitable because they have already occurred.

Our task in this chapter is to extend and apply our earlier discussion (Chapters 1 and 2) of the sources and directions of change in whole societies, first from internal and then from external causes. A category of societal change of major consequence in the contemporary world, the "modernization" of traditional societies, is singled out for more intense scrutiny in the following chapter.

CHANGE-PRODUCING TENSIONS

Although societies may be viewed as interdependent systems of social action, our discussion to this point has provided ample warning that, like any scientific construct or model, the closeness of fit to the actual course of events is a legitimate question and not to be silenced by presumptions made for analytical purposes. If roles and rules were completely interdependent, we should have to assume that societies would be highly resistant to change, whether of internal or external origin. We should also face the dilemma noted earlier that actual changes would have to be either "trivial," having essentially "no" significant consequences, or "tragic," owing to the reverberations of change through a tightly interlocked system. When we operate with a somewhat looser model of social systems, we can countenance partial or small-scale changes that are not of substantial significance for the structure of society. We can then also permit ourselves to ask about the probability that specified internal changes will have consequences for the more encompassing system, and about the form and degree of such consequences.

Aggregate Effects of Small-Scale Changes

It is even possible that small-scale changes, properly viewed as having slight structural signifiance where they occur, have, by their generality, substantial aggregate effects. For example, a change from a modal (most frequent) number of children per family of two to a mode of three, may be rather insignificant for family structure, and only at the level where the nuances of interpersonal relations are to be considered. Such a change would not materially affect the structural and institutional characteristics of the "small family system." Yet the aggregate effect of such a change—and this is a real example drawn from the experience of the Western World following World War II—profoundly affects rates of population growth, the needs for schools and other services, prospective size of the labor force, the demand for consumer goods, and, eventually the destiny of traffic and residential settlement.

The first strain or tension that is predictive of change, thus, is that between the "part" and the "whole", the somewhat specialized system of action and its consequences for the society in which it is located. This may be put in a somewhat more general form. Society, being a looser system than any complex biological organism, permits ranges of "structural substitutability" consistent with the requisites or conditions for its survival as a system. Within some range, change in the way particular functions are fulfilled may make no difference. Beyond that range, changes in the consequences of patterned behavior will have wider ramifications, both with regard to other patterns and with regard to the way and degree to which the society's requisites for survival are in fact met, if indeed they are met. (A society may cease to exist as a self-subsistent entity, or may change so radically and discontinuously that it would be difficult to identify it as the same system.)

Let us take two more examples from the field of demography, the study of the structure and changes in population. Sexual recruitment, obviously a condition for persistence of a society, is normally and normatively entrusted to decentralized social units—families. The basic structural features of a society may be little affected by rather wide "cross-sectional" variability in the performance of these units; that is, the number of children produced by the several families may range rather widely as long as the aggregate number does not vary much and is adequate to offset prevailing levels of mortality. Even changes in the aggregate of fresh recruits may not be significant if the changes are not sharp and rapid and if they fluctuate rather than show a persistent trend. But suppose—and again this is a true condition, reflecting the situation in most of the underdeveloped areas—that high aggregate birth rates are no longer offset by high death rates, as the latter have yielded to public health measures and the improvement and spread of drugs and medical services. The approximate "balance" is thus upset, and efforts to improve levels of living are hampered because there are more people to support instead of a constant number existing at higher levels. We thus encounter a problem of "lead" and "lag," with widespread ramifications for economic planning and quite possibly for public policy in attempting to close the gap by encouraging voluntary family limitation.[1]

The other demographic example relates to the downward course of birth rates in the Western World for a century or more ending with the Great Depression of the 1930's. During virtually the entire period and apparently in all countries exhibiting the downward trend, the decline was seemingly led by urban populations, and certainly by the more highly educated and prosperous families. Thus there was a persistent *negative* correlation between the number of children and the family's financial ability to afford them. One consequence of this situation was that, despite the real inequalities of opportunity that differences in wealth and education imply for children clever enough to be born into privileged families, those families as a whole did not in effect reproduce themselves, and thus there were "vacancies" to be filled by youths from poorer economic circumstances.[2] In a real sense the change in fertility behavior aided in *stabilizing* systems that included individual mobility and equality of opportunity among their articulated values. The tale is not all told, however. The post-Depression birth-rate recovery occurred mainly among those groups with the lowest previous fertility—the educated and prosperous urban families. For middle- and upper-income groups the number of children is *positively* related to income or socio-economic status.[3] Although some other trends such as the extension of educational benefits at nominal cost are consistent with the ideal of increasing equality of opportunity, for the foreseeable future the implications of current fertility differentials in the Western World are somewhat dampening the rate of upward mobility between generations.

The Way Functions Are Performed

The point of departure for these illustrations was the way in which an essential function—in these cases, sexual recruitment—affects a system. In fact, by dealing with demographic changes we have also introduced considerations of magnitude, and that leads to a theoretical

1. Ansley J. Coale and Edgar M. Hoover, *Population Growth and Economic Development in Low Income Countries* (Princeton: Princeton University Press, 1958). For a brief general statement, see Kenneth E. Boulding, *A Primer on Social Dynamics* (New York: Free Press, 1970), pp. 11–12.

2. See Elbridge Sibley, "Some Demographic Clues to Stratification," *American Sociological Review* (1942), 7:322–30.

3. See Clyde V. Kiser, "Differential Fertility in the United States," in National Bureau of Economic Research, *Demographic and Economic Change in Developed Countries* (Princeton: Princeton University Press, 1960), pp. 77–113; Raymond W. Mack, *Transforming America: Patterns of Social Change* (New York: Random House, 1967) Chap. 3, "Births, Deaths, and Families: Traits and Trends."

problem that is fraught with hazards but must still be faced as bravely as possible. The conception of "requisite" functions for the persistence of societies[4] tends to encourage (but does not require) a "plus or minus" or "all or none" manner of thinking. By definition, a requisite function must be performed if the system is to persist. Yet this definitional proposition does not prohibit considerations of approximation and degree. A function may be fulfilled but at a less than an ideal level if we have some standard of value or criterion of efficiency against which to measure it. Biological survival based on high fertility that compensates for high mortality is clearly less efficient than a balance maintained by low fertility that offsets low mortality. High mortality, and especially infant mortality, spends the system's scarce economic resources on investments that yield little or no return. In most societies death is a negative value for most people in most circumstances, so that the value standard does not have to be invented by the interpreter. For that is the principal hazard in this line of argument— namely, that the *degree* of functional performance may surreptitiously entrap the analyst into constructing a set of ideal value standards other than those that he observes, and then attempting to assess performance against these essentially "external" standards. The line between that improper behavior and the identification of patterns of action that may imperil the persistence of the system as specified is often subtle. Identifying disfunctional patterns need not involve a value judgment, for perhaps from some ethical standpoint the system ought not to survive.

An example of another type of societal function may help to clarify the question of degree of fulfillment. A social system depends for its existence on the maintenance of order—on predictable conduct and conformity with norms of conduct and values. Now clearly the most efficient system would be one in which everyone or at least every adult was solely self-disciplined by virtue of his having completely and consistently "internalized" the codes of behavior. Yet no known society is lacking in some incidence of "crime" or nonconformity, nor without some unknown incidence of overt conformity because of the threat of external sanctions rather than because of the dictates of conscience. It is thus surely proper to speak of the way *and the degree* to which the order-maintaining function is performed, and changes in either are likely to have wide ramifications.

Crime rates may be taken as one crude and approximate indication of the incidence of nonconformity with the established order, various kinds of "internal war" as another. Crime rates are not likely to be very accurate for comparisons between societies, and in fact present all sorts of difficulties even when applied to individual societies and through

4. See Marion J. Levy, Jr., *The Structure of Society* (Princeton: Princeton University Press, 1952).

time. Nevertheless, our interest at this point is less methodologically sophisticated. Crime rates, however crude, give an approximate indication of the departures from perfection in the maintenance of order. And criminal activities further illustrate the way in which a society's tensions display dynamic properties, and are likely to have further repercussions. Sutherland[5] discusses the way in which the technology of professional crime and the technology of detection and apprehension of criminals exhibit a kind of highly unstable set of competitive relations. The *order characteristics* of a complex society exhibit steady changes in the ways of handling disorder. And the needed resources, ranging from the development of technological instruments, through tax allocations, to the forms and processes of municipal administration are considerably affected by the interplay between the "good guys" and the "bad guys."

What is being argued and illustrated here is that various forms of small-scale changes that influence the exact ways in which social functions are fulfilled may well fall within some tolerance range of variability in a loose system where alternatives are possible; but that a *system* does indeed exist and therefore that these changes may well be really consequential. Obviously it is easier to detect the difference between mere optional vacillation and "significant" change after an event has occurred, but that is scarcely a worthwhile scientific (as distinct from historical) enterprise, unless cases yield predictive principles. The fact that changes may not be significant is no excuse for the failure to determine the dimensions and boundaries of really consequential alterations.

Tracing out the probable consequences of *given* changes in the major structural or functional aspects of societies—recruitment, socialization, production, protection, order, and so forth—has proceeded rather far, but is by no means complete. Yet that task is somewhat less challenging than to make the "initial" changes themselves problematical rather than given. We have rejected uniform "determinisms," which would make the matter simple but wrong. This does not necessarily imply the alternative of equal probability. Though pluralistic, our analysis as sketched in Chapter 1 is not completely latitudinarian. It does identify unequal probabilities in the sources and rates of change within a society and thus involves conceptions of "leads" and "lags." The principal sources of change-producing tensions are recapitulated later in this section.

Types of Autonomous Changes

However, another question must be considered, and that is whether certain standard components of cultures and societies are especially au-

---

5. See Edwin H. Sutherland and Donald R. Cressey, *Principles of Criminology*, 5th ed. (Chicago: Lippincott, 1955), pp. 225–26.

tonomous. Such relative autonomy would have two implications for the analysis of social change: relatively high and long insulation from the effects of other systemic changes, but correlatively, fairly "easy" autonomous changes, including those of external origin, owing to the meager links to the balance of the system. Although the evidence relating to the independent variability of some standard components of social systems is extremely sketchy, it does appear that aesthetic canons and forms provide one such manifestation and that strictly super-empirical components of religious belief represent another. To repeat, if these hypotheses are correct, it would follow that aesthetic forms and super-empirical beliefs would be only slightly affected by other social transformations, but by the same token might well exhibit changes that have little to do with their immediate social environment and in fact possibly are a result of external influence. The loose connection with other role structures and ordinary patterns of behavior means that relatively autonomous change might occur without a kind of "systemic resistance" deriving from interlocking patterns. This hypothetical situation is illustrated in Fig. 16.

Although this line of speculation runs contrary to the major current theoretical positions in anthropology and sociology, which emphasize and possibly exaggerate systematic relations, it is consistent with rather impressive historical experience.

ALTHOUGH CONTEMPORARY ART FORMS have greatly multiplied and diversified, "classical" forms have by no means been abandoned. Current fashion in art is highly volatile, but attempts to correlate those changes with other social changes appear futile.

EVEN SEEMINGLY DISTINCTIVE and traditional art forms, such as Chinese water colors and painting, have been in fact strongly influenced by borrowing from "outside."

CHRISTIAN THEOLOGY, as distinct from Christian ethics and prescriptions for conduct or forms of religious organization, has endured for nearly two millennia despite vast secular changes in the social environment.

THE GREAT "MISSIONARY" RELIGIONS such as Buddhism, Islam, and Christianity have at times spread rapidly through cultures and societies otherwise highly diverse.

This is not to argue that these components of cultures or societies have *no* connections with their social settings, but only that their autonomy is greater than is true of most common structural features of societies. We have only to remind ourselves of the Soviet attempt to impose "socialist realism" on art and to foster atheism as a religious orientation to realize that the insulation is by no means total. Yet the incomplete success of both attempts at doctrinal purity provides some additional support to the theory of partial autonomy. Sorokin has criticized

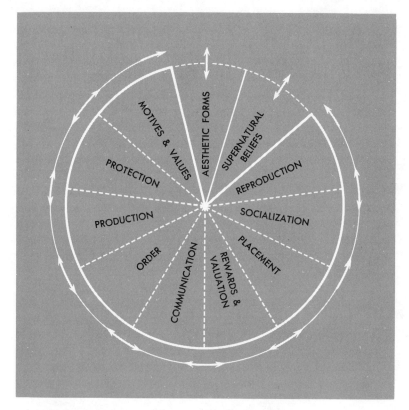

Figure 16. Diagrammatic representation of closely inter-related social functions and of relatively autonomous aspects of culture.

this line of argument, citing his own voluminous materials, attempting to relate art forms, ideologies, and "systems of truth" to major cultural types.[6] Sorokin's evidence, however, is limited to Western civilization, and the relationships he claims are simply not very persuasive. To take but one example, Sorokin attempted to correlate art forms with his cultural types, expecting nudity to be related to *sensate* ("truth of senses") cultures and not to *ideational* ("truth of faith") cultures. In fact, however, there is considerable nudity in religious paintings.

What would account for these special cases of persistence and change? It appears that their relative immunity to intricate systemic

6. Pitirim A. Sorokin, *Sociological Theories of Today* (New York: Harper & Row, 1966), pp. 610–11. (See also Sorokin, *Social and Cultural Dynamics* (New York: American Book, 1937–41), 4 vols.; one-vol. ed.: Boston: Porter Sargent, 1957.)

linkage[7] derives from the circumstance that neither aesthetic canons nor supernatural beliefs are subject to rational calculation in the ordinary sense nor to scientific or experiential modification. There may be some limited aspects of other essentially cultural systems, such as language and law, that share these sources of immunity but to identify them appears impossible given the current state of our knowledge.

Environmental Adjustment

The theory of a *persistent environmental challenge,* proposed in Chapter I, provides the basis for the possible acceptability of chance technical innovations as well as the possibility of purposeful problem solving. The argument, it will be recalled, was to the effect that societies are never found in a state of "frictionless" adjustment with their natural settings. As long as at least part of the forces of nature remain uncontrolled and as long as sheer physical survival is uncertain (and man's mortality assures that it will be, sooner or later), there will be a source of tension between the ideal and the actual.

What this means for changes in the structure of societies may be seen at two levels: (a) the probability of technical innovations, which will alter but not resolve the character of the environmental challenge, and (b) the "secondary effects" of alterations in the society's technological base. The big shifts resulting from technological change are of course the most obvious ones: the domestication of animals, the invention of agriculture, the use of irrigation, the steam or internal combustion engine. Yet a relatively minor technological shift, an improvement rather than an invention, such as the substitution of steel plows for wooden ones, may have far-reaching effects.[8] White argues that as steel plows came to be adopted in Europe beginning around the tenth century, the weight of the tools encouraged the substitution of horses for oxen—with a long train of consequences, including the whole technology of harnessing and the selective breeding of horses for specialized uses. The deeper furrows cut by the steel plow increased soil productivity and were a major factor in changes in land allotments and distributions.[9]

It is indeed easy to trace out trains of consequence of given technological changes. What is critical is the ability to assess the probability of such changes in the first place. If we wish to generalize for all societies

---

7. See Charles P. Loomis, *Social Systems* (Princeton: Van Nostrand, 1960), especially pp. 32–35.

8. See Lynn White, Jr., *Medieval Technology and Social Change* (Oxford: Clarendon Press, 1962), pp. 41–69.

9. Ibid., pp. 69–76.

and all times, we can only rely on the environmental challenge as providing both the probability of problem-solving innovations and the probability that at least some of these will in fact be accepted, with further consequences of the sort that we have noted with respect to the plow.

Let us examine the environmental challenge and its influence in a rather different context of social behavior, that of "magic." Malinowski[10] drew a clear analytical distinction between *religion*, as the modes of orientation to ultimate values and superempirical goals, and *magic*, the use of superempirical or at least nonrational means for the achievement of empirical ends. Now, contrary to Lévy-Bruhl,[11] for example, Malinowski convincingly argued that religion and magic in combination do not exhaust the content of "primitive mentality." Primitive societies do use rational techniques of production, construction, healing, and so on. But the techniques available often fall short of the desired reliability of results. The best-built fishing canoes may swamp in storms, and the fish may have left the place at sea where they had been found before. Careful planting and tending of gardens may come to naught if the weather is adverse or the crops suffer the depredations of insects and animals. "Folk remedies" for the ill may still not save the patient's life. It is the gap between rational control and the need for control that magic fills.

This view of the function of magic has received fairly general acceptance. Its significance for our analysis of social change is that *technology*— the use of reliable empirical knowledge and rational techniques to achieve specific empirical goals—and magic are evidently competitive. Although belief in the efficacy of magic may well, here and there, provide effective resistance to new technical alternatives, the evidence is fairly overwhelming that as a general rule superior technology wins out.

Two further points must be mentioned in this connection, however. Magic is not a peculiarity of the social behavior of unlettered savages. The Malinowski theory is *very* general, and applies to any circumstance where there is a gap between rational technique and completely effective prediction and control. It follows that even modern man may be expected to have what a rationalistic culture would designate as "superstitions." Occupational magic abounds where work is dangerous for life and limb or where outcomes are uncertain but important both to the individual and the collectivity, as in professional sports. Weather magic is common, and healing magic also. The environmental challenge, in other words, is nowhere completely suppressed by effective human mastery. Yet the

10. Bronislaw Malinowski, "Culture," in *Encyclopedia of the Social Sciences* (New York: Macmillan, 1930), see also his *Magic, Science, and Religion* (Glencoe, Ill.: Free Press, 1948).

11. See, for example, Lucien Lévy-Bruhl, *Primitive Mentality* (New York: Macmillan, 1923).

search for rational mastery does erode the need for magical practices or their particular form and context.

The other point to be stressed is that the distinction between religion and magic is analytical. Concrete religious systems tend to go beyond a concern with, say, faith in God and belief in man's immortality, and to exhibit concern for man's mundane problems. Thus divine intercession in the course of human events may be sought. This is precisely magic. The association of magic and religion in concrete systems of belief and practice tends to give magical solutions more protection against rational attack than if magic were simply "incorrect technology." Yet even in this situation, though the evidence is not completely firm, it appears that both the incidence and the contexts of resort to ritual solutions or the seeking of special intercession change as rational technology alters and expands.

The probabilities of technical innovation vary, though, in time and space, and one major source of such variability is the unequal extensity and intensity of a rational orientation to the environment. Though such an orientation is certainly never lacking, even in traditionalistic tribal societies, the kinds and degrees of applicability of a problem-solving approach appear to be quite unequal. In the Western World, the great emphasis on deliberate mastery of nature is commonly traced to the Renaissance and especially to the scientific revolution of the sixteenth century. White, on the basis of his studies of medieval technology, places the origins much earlier (the tenth century or before). Noting that with the heavy plow, ". . . the standard of land distribution ceased to be the needs of a family and became the ability of a power-engine to till the earth," he adds, "No more fundamental change in the idea of man's relation to the soil can be imagined: once man had been part of nature; now he became her exploiter. . . . Man and nature are now two things, and man is master."[12]

Although White no doubt exaggerates the discontinuity with the past, for the "rational spirit" was certainly evident in the Greco-Roman world and elsewhere, Sorokin is undoubtedly correct in emphasizing the "fluctuations" in emphasis on science and technology.[13] A major feature of the modern world, a feature to which we shall return in our discussion of change in industrial societies, is that the rational orientation is pervasive and a major basis for deliberate change in virtually every aspect of man's concerns.[14]

12. White, *Medieval Technology and Social Change*, pp. 56–57.

13. See Sorokin, *Social and Cultural Dynamics*, one-vol. ed., especially Chaps. 13, 14, and 23.

14. See Wilbert E. Moore, "Introduction" in Moore (ed.), *Technology and Social Change* (Chicago: Quadrangle Books, 1972).

The linking of "science and technology" is itself a very modern phenomenon, according to Kuhn.[15] He doubts the interplay between abstract principles and practical applications prior to the nineteenth century. Since then, more as a consequence than as a cause of the Industrial Revolution, a kind of uneasy and not always harmoniously organized junction between science and technology has been rather common. Kuhn, however, notes that in terms of attitude and method, rather than results, the link was established "at least a century earlier."[16]

The extension of rational orientations, called elsewhere "the rise of the rational spirit,"[17] has invaded fields as traditionally nonrational as mate selection, occupational choice, and modes of social organization. Even with regard to the role of religion in human affairs, the "rational spirit" takes the form of *secularization*, the substitution of nonreligious beliefs and practices for religious ones. Although secularization is a many-faceted development, its significance in the present context is the emphasis on rational rather than traditional or supernatural solutions to the many situations of risk and uncertainty to which the human condition is still subject.

The Problem of Order

The failure of perfection in "social control," we have noted, is a universal feature of human societies. It is yet another example of the lack of correspondence between the ideal and the actual in social systems. The argument with regard to this probable source of change in societies is closely analogous to the influence of the environmental challenge. In both cases the general lack of ideal solutions is universal and enduring, although the particular contexts and degrees of adjustment are variable through space and time. In both cases the disparity between the ideal and the actual provides the probability of innovation and the probability that some innovations, whether deliberate or by chance, will be acceptable.

The history of what we may designate as "social technology" is far less well documented than the history of inventions designed to control the physical, chemical, or biological world. Such devices as the majority

15. Thomas S. Kuhn, "Comment," on paper by Irving H. Siegel in National Bureau of Economic Research, *The Rate and Direction of Inventive Activity: Economic and Social Factors* (Princeton: Princeton University Press, 1962), pp. 450–57.

16. Ibid., p. 454, note 4.

17. See Wilbert E. Moore, "Measurement of Organizational and Institutional Implications of Changes in Productive Technology," in International Social Science Council, *Social, Economic and Technological Change* (Paris, 1958), pp. 229–59. Reprinted in Moore, *Order and Change* (New York: Wiley, 1967), Chap. 4.

vote for reaching collective decisions, the minority being bound to comply, have had far-reaching consequences for social control but cannot be effectively dated. It is probably far less old in human history than the hereditary principle of selection of political rulers, but the statement cannot be made with absolute confidence. Even "bureaucracy," the complex administrative organization that recruits and promotes on technical or "universalistic" grounds and maintains a division of labor and function coordinated by graded authority, is not wholly modern. There were major elements of such organizations in the governments of ancient empires, in both civil and military activities.[18] Even the rule of law, and especially the control of the destructive effects of the use of force, are of great antiquity. Similarly, the aid of secular authority by appeals to divine will, with or without a special class of religious officials, has been the general rule in human societies, and it is questionable (and partly a matter of definition) whether it is absent in any modern society.

Yet clearly not all forms of social control have existed "from the beginning." In the political sphere—properly speaking—that is, the formal structure of the state—it is doubtful that a specific and specialized legislative function existed prior to the Roman era, and that form of control virtually disappeared until the rise of the parliamentary states with the breakdown of feudalism. A specialized judicial system for applying the law to particular cases seems to have had a similar course.

We are on more secure ground in recent history, partly because of written records of explicit attempts to solve various problems of order, and partly no doubt because of the steady extension of the rational orientation to the social as well as environmental realms of human uncertainty. The range of control devices and the rate of invention of new ones is truly impressive in the contemporary world. From covert advertising touching subconscious motives to the techniques of indirect rule of colonial territories, from the indulgence of status-seeking to the terror of "brainwashing," from the alternative principles of child-rearing to the trapping of professional criminals through tax laws—the inventiveness of modern man in the exercise of power and the reduction of deviant behavior is truly impressive. Yet the problems of order appear to multiply at least as fast as the attempted solutions, mainly because of changes in other major aspects of social systems and their relations.

Social Revolution

Sharply *revolutionary* changes in modes of social control are also to be found with remarkable frequency in human societies. Of the various

---

18. See Shmuel N. Eisenstadt, *The Political Systems of Empires* (New York: Free Press, 1963).

forms of "internal war," revolutions constitute the greatest challenge to the principles of social change.

We may distinguish several types of disturbance of the social order in the formal structure of the state.

1. "Ordinary" criminal action, violating some part of the legal codes but not essentially challenging other parts. Clearly, the extent of the challenge is variable, both as measured by the impact on the constituted system and by the frequency of offenses. Thus an organized criminal syndicate may become a kind of internal, rebellious state. Similarly, a high incidence of crimes of personal violence is likely to make ordinary social life precarious, even though the crimes are unorganized and not extensive in terms of the range of laws violated.

2. The "rebellion" which is localized and commonly directed at a particular grievance. Again the lines are not completely distinct, as the rebellion may in fact be an abortive revolution. In fact, Leach[19] has argued persuasively that most violent political activity in human societies is rebellious rather than revolutionary, because of the general absence (particularly in many non-literate cultures) of a highly centralized government that could be overthrown.

3. The *coup d' état*, which although representing an illegal usurpation of power that may be accompanied by some violence, does not result in major changes in the structure of government or in the legal bases of other social institutions.

4. The "revolution," which is violent, engages a considerable portion of the population, and results in a change in the structure of government, the legal codes relating to other major social functions, and the grounds on which officials base their right to govern.

Theories of revolution abound, and differ widely. Sorokin attempts the widest possible historical and comparative coverage, and concludes that revolutions are most probable in "transitional" periods with respect to major cultural values and the fundamental bases of social relationships.[20] Hopper offers as a general hypothesis: "The emergence of a numerically significant, economically powerful, and intellectually informed marginal group is one of the earliest indicators of impending revolution."[21] Although Hopper's hypothesis fits well several Latin American cases that he discusses, it is more likely to predict disorder than

19.   Edmund R. Leach, *Political Systems of Highland Burma* (Cambridge: Harvard University Press, 1954).

20.   Sorokin, *Social and Cultural Dynamics*, one-vol. ed., Chap. 35.

21.   Rex D. Hopper, "Cybernation, Marginality, and Revolution," in Irving Louis Horowitz (ed.) *The New Sociology* (New York: Oxford University Press, 1964), Chap. 19; quotation from p. 313.

revolution.[22] The more complex and multi-dimensional the bases of social differentiation, the less likely is a clear-cut confrontation. To take a simple example, the early stages of industrialization are marked by a radical polarity between the managers and the managed in the modernized sector. Marx perceived this correctly, and made a totally false extrapolation of inclusive, class conflict. Early polarization characterizes only a relatively small segment of the social structure, and the more traditional differentiation rests on other bases. This duality prevents any strict and comprehensive set of social divisions. By the time that modernization has affected most of the social order its typical status gradations have multiplied, and status itself has become multidimensional. Thus revolution is not the *normal* consequence of modernization, though under certain combinations of circumstances it is not unknown. The contemporary speed of sharp rises in aspirations, combined with relative slowness in economic improvements, greatly increases the probability of revolution in "new nations."

Polarization, then, is the key indicator of incipient revolution. It is, however, only, an indicator and no more causes revolution than the thermometer causes temperature. But what we are looking for, taking account of other and more fundamental harbingers that will be noted presently, is the transition from fractionation and shifting coalitions to broadly divisive and enduring coalitions.

What are the more fundamental determinants of revolution? Certainly one is an objective and apparent deterioration in economic well-being or political rights. The deterioration may be relative as well as absolute, as when the rich get richer and the poor, if anything, poorer.

In particular, revolutions are probable wherever structural changes in the legally sanctioned distribution of power and social rewards have been slight or retrogressive. Thus the Republic of South Africa and the Rhodesias are safe bets for revolution, and most Latin American countries are odds-on favorites. It is extremely difficult for an entrenched élite to perceive that its days are numbered unless it makes concessions. The plea is for time, yet poor use is made of time at hand. Indeed, the early perception of threat most commonly leads to repressive rather than conciliatory measures, and thus an acceleration of the process of polarization. A somewhat "integrated" ideology is formed, but it still contains rather arbitrarily selected differentiators ("Oh, you like spinach? You must be one of those communists."). The world of everyday experience becomes simplified, if restrictive, for a time, whether the revolutionary movement succeeds or fails. Partisan indentification defines

---

22. The remainder of this paragraph and the following three adapted from Wilbert E. Moore, "Predicting Discontinuities in Social Change, *American Sociological Review*, June, 1964, 29:331–38.

nearly all social action. A balanced, or criss-crossing, or indecisive view is regarded by both polar camps with simple hostility.

Although some theories of the *course* of revolutions emphasize the restoration of major structural features of societies—either in their original state, or along their prior trends of change[23]—there is no basis for denying that revolutions do institute enduring changes. At the very least, the characteristic power-and-resource balances among various structural components of societies are likely to be durably altered, especially the characteristic tensions of the system and the ways they are managed.

THE TENSIONS OF INEQUALITY

Social differentiation, the assignment of various roles and positions to different members of a social system, is clearly a universal characteristic of human societies. The minimum basis for such differentiation is biological: the realities of age, sex, and the uneven distribution of physiological and mental talents in any substantial population. No society stops with such bases of differentiation, adding at least position in kinship systems and usually a variety of others to the list.

Both differential positions and differential role performances are universal sources of inequality: in rewards and punishments ranging from mere informal approval or disapproval to the unequal allocation of such scarce and valued resources as property and power. The so-called "functional" interpretation of social inequality (inappropriately made equivalent to "social stratification") put forward by Davis and Moore[24] argued that positions must be unequally rewarded because of differences in their functional importance and differences in talent within populations. This view has been challenged,[25] particularly (and correctly) because of its neglect of the "disfunctions" of *stratification*, properly speaking, which entail the formation of "classes" or "strata" that provide unequal opportunities for children, even if these opportunities are "open" on the basis of performance and achievement.

In this controversy, where the issues are not always clearly joined, no one questions the universality of inequality and even of some form and degree of stratification. The questions that remain in dispute are: the significance of the agreement that differential compliance with ideal norms

23. See Crane Brinton, *Anatomy of Revolution* (New York: Norton, 1938).

24. See Kingsley Davis and Wilbert E. Moore, "Some Principles of Stratification," *American Sociological Review*, April, 1945, 10:242–49.

25. See Melvin M. Tumin, "On Inequality" *American Sociological Review*, February, 1963, 28:19–26.

will and must be differentially valued, and the question whether positions (as distinct from performance) *must* be differentially rewarded by allocations of power and property.

The dispute has aided in clarifying one matter of present concern, and that is the dynamic aspect of any system of inequality—that is, social stratification. On the evidence, it appears extremely unlikely (a cautious way of saying "impossible") that any mode of rewarding positions unequally and any mode of determining access to those positions would be so firmly institutionalized that those persons most injured would accept the justice of their fate. What this statement says in less technical language is that the rules governing assignments to positions and their unequal rewards, and the values that "justify" these rules, will not be accepted as totally valid by those who are thereby excluded.

Stratification systems may in fact endure for considerable periods without causing rebellion or revolt, but because of the differential distribution of power (including knowledge), this is neither surprising nor quite to the point. The critical question must be, how will the poor, the powerless, the denigrated members of the system react to possible alternatives. For "complete" institutionalization, alternatives should be rejected as unthinkable, and that nowhere appears to be the situation.

There is, however, a qualification that must be entered in the predictive pattern. It is not always the most downtrodden members of the system that lead movements of protest or form the spearheads of discontent. Rather, the overt manifestations of disenchantment are likely to occur among those who have not fared badly but also not well. Even Marx, whose capacity as a social analyst was often betrayed by his political ideology and whose prophetic vision of the polarization of class interests in industrial societies was exactly and totally wrong, understood the difference between "leading elements" and what he properly dismissed as the *Lumpenproletariat.*[26] This characteristic of protest by those who have escaped the very lowest positions has been repeatedly observed in the newly developing areas of the world,[27] and we get from this evidence a kind of cross-sectional confirmation of dynamic processes. The "relative deprivation" of those fairly fully incorporated into the values associated with new modes of social placement and mobility, but thereby more envious of full success than their less fortunate compatriots, provides

26. See Karl Marx, "The Class Struggles in France, 1848 to 1850," in Karl Marx and Frederick Engels, *Selected Works*, Vol. 1 (Moscow: Foreign Language Publishing House, 1962), pp. 118–242, especially p. 155; also in the same edition, "The Eighteenth Brumaire of Louis Bonaparte," pp. 243–344, especially pp. 294–95.

27. Clark Kerr and others, *Industrialism and Industrial Man* (Cambridge: Harvard University Press, 1960), Chap. 8.

the explanatory key to the source of discontent in systems of social inequality.

We do not have to invent, or stipulate, external alternatives, however. Discordant principles of social placement are likely to highlight the discontent incipient in any system of inequality, but even those systems elaborately rationalized exhibit evidence of strictly internal tensions. The Indian caste system, for example, has shown over the long term a fairly substantial degree of unrest and the repeated occurrence of maneuvers aimed at changing relative positions.

The Marxist doctrine that "all history is the history of class struggle"[28] is only partially accurate. Its most elementary defect is distortion, for history is marked by man's struggle against "nature" and against "sin" also. But its subtler error is implicit: that somehow, by the establishment of a different social system, this kind of dynamic tension will be removed. Like the Utopian Socialists that he criticized, Marx made the fundamental blunder of thinking that an ideal society is possible. If inequality tends to encounter severe problems of equity, so would an egalitarian system. To assume that a system of undifferentiated equality and rewards would be more stable (or equitable) than a differential system is pure prejudice. "The practice of equal rewards for unequal performance does not immediately recommend itself as either functionally or ethically superior to the contrary scandal of unequal rewards for equal performance."[29]

The question of the unequal distribution of power and various "awards" in societies thus appears as a special case of the general problem of order. By no means all challenges to established power distributions or forms of government are class-oriented, or directly concerned with relative social position, except in the definitional sense that a challenge to power is aimed at somehow changing the exercise of power. Some challenges clearly derive from simple disaffection from the prevailing norms as evidenced by the pursuit of special interests (for example, theft of property) at the expense of others. Other challenges simply dispute the merits or competence of power-holders and would seek to replace them with others. This is probably the most common form of "insurrection," whether violent or not. Yet it remains true that one major source of tension, and therefore of potential change, in societies rests on disbelief in the existing rationales for evident inequality and the substitution of others. It is doubtful that anyone anywhere truly believes in complete social equality,

28. Karl Marx and Frederick Engels, *Manifesto of the Communist Party* (Chicago: Kerr, 1906).

29. Moore, "But Some Are More Equal Than Others," *American Sociological Review*, February, 1963, 28:13–18.

but it is equally doubtful that any existing system of inequality has anything approximating unanimous support.

ACCULTURATION

The term "acculturation" has come to mean the transfer of "cultural" or social elements from one society to another. As such the phenomena included are extremely diverse, ranging, say, from a relatively isolated adoption of a foreign technical term into a language lacking any equivalent, to the virtually total transformation of social systems under the impact of massive "external" political influence or the provision of preferable models of economic production and social organization.

Despite a substantial amount of interest in inter-system transfers, an interest particularly displayed by anthropologists prior to the contemporary rapid and large-scale changes in most formerly primitive societies,[30] it is only honest to say that most of the work in this field has been trivial. Save only for the recent work on the "social consequences of 'development,' " to which our attention turns in the following chapter, the studies of acculturation have suffered from either an excess of simplicity—treating variables in isolation—or an excess of complexity—treating cultures or social systems as so extensively and autonomously integrated that external influences were viewed as either fundamentally altering the entire system or unimportant.

Contacts between cultures or societies are in the statistical sense "normal," although both the variety and the frequency of such contacts have been quite different in time and place. If we take a crude index of frequency together with number of people involved, the leading modes of cultural contact might rank something like the following:

> Imperialism, including both colonization and indirect rule
> Other wars, conquests, and military occupations
> Missionary religions, which might be called "religious imperialism"
> Mass migration, such as the movement of populations within the Eurasian land mass
> "Individual" migration, such as the Atlantic migration and the Chinese in Southeast Asia
> Economic trade
> Tourism
> Transported labor (for example, through slavery or indenture and penal deportations)
> Transfers of knowledge
> Diplomacy, indirect contacts, formal communications

---

30. For a review of the relevant literature see Wilbert E. Moore, *Industrialization and Labor* (Ithaca: Cornell University Press, 1951), pp. 178–99.

No great confidence can be placed in the exact order of these forms of contact. They do, however, indicate something of the range and diversity of the relations between societies. They also suggest that even prior to the modern era enduring isolation must have been rather exceptional.

The "principles of acculturation" lend themselves to a series of two-variable propositions, moderately persuasive but largely untested. The reason for the meager state of proof of these allegations is simple: the explicit or implicit assumption of *ceteris paribus*—other things being equal—does not generally prevail in nature. Carefully designed comparative studies—for example, the degree of homogeneity among widely diverse post-colonial cultures arising from common colonial administration and influence from the colonizing power—remain to be made.

Subject to these severe restrictions, the writers on acculturation suggest that the transfer of cultural items is correlated with:

Their simplicity
Consistency with existing values
Prestige of the bearers of novelty
An already changing situation in the receiving culture
Lack of close "integration" of the receiving system, as exemplified for example by the importance of disaffected elements
The extent and continuity of contact

The variant of technological determinism that argues that tools and techniques are most readily transferable is consistent with the theory of "environmental challenge," but must not be exaggerated into a unique prediction. A manifestly better way of producing goods or curing illness may indeed be "readily" acceptable, even at some cost (for example, the displacement of local tool-making artisans or traditional "curers"). Yet the better way also may include forms of social organization, legal codes, and even systems of religious beliefs.

Again, a monistic approach will simply not do. Three examples of major and widespread "diffusions" of fairly complex and "non-material" cultural systems serve to restrain the naive view that tools are always more readily acceptable than ideas. One, as we have seen, is the successful spread of the world's great missionary religions—Buddhism, Christianty and Islam. If we regard communism also as a missionary religion, its spread in relatively underdeveloped areas precisely contradicts its own doctrines, and yields one of the grosser paradoxes of our time. In a sense the theology of communism appears independent of its claims to scientific truth, claims that emphasize the independent, almost irrelevant quality of ideology as growing out of the material conditions and economic structure of society.

A second example of the diffusion of a complex "non-material" system is that of the imposition and survival of the Code Napoleon as the foundation of civil, administrative, and criminal law in much of continental Western Europe to this day.

A third example is also of great importance in the contemporary world: the nearly universal acceptance, at least by political officials and spokesmen, of the doctrine of economic development. In fact communism is simply one alternative type of this doctrine. Now although the quest for economic growth appears materialistic, it is precisely the economy, and its associated technology, that are lagging and ideology that is leading. "A worldly doctrine, it is the single most successful conversion movement in the history of ideological diffusion."[31]

No single theory appears likely to explain three such disparate cases of major cultural diffusion. Aside from the suggestion that religious theologies, like aesthetic canons, represent special cases of relatively autonomous persistence, change, and diffusion, a further interpretation may be offered. It may perhaps be argued that it was the very complexity of the religious systems that aided their acceptance, for they combined fairly elaborate and "sophisticated" theology—a metaphysical cosmology, a conception of the divine order of the universe and the nature of divine or supernatural forces, explanations of life and death and good and evil— with a specific religious organization and procedures for handling life's problems. It is notable that the successes have chiefly been scored in competition with much less "complete" religious systems, and not primarily with other complex ones.

Although the system of Roman law was originally imposed rather than voluntarily borrowed (but this was also true of part of the spread of Christianity and Islam), its persistence may again perhaps be traced to its completeness and "logical" order. In this case the evidence appears consistent with the theory that political order is always incomplete and problematical, providing the basis for innovation in systems of control.

The doctrine of economic growth, although many of the consequences of its implementation are inconsistent with traditional values and structures, is consistent with certain values that turn out to be virtually universal in human societies. Despite the emphasis on the diversity of cultural values and social systems, a "relativistic" view that was the fairly standard theoretical position of anthropologists and sociologists for something like the first four decades of this century, the economists who subscribed to the view that certain wants are universal turned out to have been more nearly correct. Given the option, or even the knowledge of alternatives existing elsewhere, it turns out that most people in most places prefer food to hunger, health to sickness, physical comfort to suf-

---

31. Wilbert E. Moore and Arnold S. Feldman (eds.), *Labor Commitment and Social Change in Developing Areas* (New York: Social Science Research Council, 1960), Preface, p. v.

fering, and life to death. Whether they also prefer work to "leisure," urban agglomeration to village life, close temporal synchronization to the uneven pace of traditional production is more doubtful, and it is at this level that difficulties arise in the process of economic development and industrialization.

Because modernization in all its ramifications is the major form of acculturation in the contemporary world, that complex process is likely to be the main source of generalizations concerning changes in societies from external sources.

One generalization applicable to the process of modernization but also to all other modes of contact is that the rate of change in any society will be highly correlated with the extent of inter-society contact. Relatively isolated tribal societies still persist in some of the less accessible areas of the world, but their number is small and dwindling.

CHAPTER 5
MODERNIZATION

The rapid incorporation of virtually every part of the world into the international political and economic "community" marks the end, or the beginning of the end, for isolated and exotic tribal communities and also for complex and archaic civilizations. In this sense, and only in this sense, the unification of the world is already nearly complete.

The process of modernization is broad, and the strands that make it up are somewhat separable one from another. In one area at one time, the problem may be defined as that of reducing illiteracy or providing potable water to urban slums or spraying mosquito-breeding swamps with chemicals to control malaria. In other places at other times, roads or hydro-electric installations may be given top priority. In still other places, or in the same places at other times, precedence may go to capital-goods industries, light consumer-goods industries, or a revamped civil service.

What is involved in modernization is a "total" transformation of a traditional or pre-modern society into the types of technology and associated social organization that characterize the "advanced," economically properous, and relatively politically stable nations of the Western World. Because so many aspects of the social order in the underdeveloped areas of the world do not conform with the models set by the advanced countries, there is room for improvement in practically any direction one looks. The definition of which problems are most urgent tends to be made by the effective political authorities, and may or may not fit what an objective social analyst would seize on as the most strategic factors for what is agreed to be the ultimate goal: a general transformation of the conditions of life and the way life is socially organized.

The problems are indeed complex, and the solutions by no means uniform for all times and all places. Communism for example offers a set of more or less rigid prescriptions for the sequence of changes in order to modernize a "backward" country. That sequence is drawn from the experience in Russia following the Bolshevik Revolution of 1917. First, agrarian populations are "sequestered" by a land reform that gains their political support or quiescence, while manifold concessions are made to existing capitalist and entrepreneurial elements in the population, under stringent political controls. As the economy recovers from revolutionary turbulence and the political leaders consolidate their power through the use of terror as well as benefits and widen their support among the new industrial wage-earners, a fully socialist regime of nationalized industries and collectivized farms is imposed. Subsequent priorities are variable and essentially pragmatic.

This kind of pattern is, on objective grounds, radically inappropriate to most of the diverse conditions of underdeveloped areas which lack the pre-Soviet Russian industrial development, the under-utilized land areas, and a quasifeudal landed aristocracy. Yet given adequate political power, the communist theory of development may be made "self-fulfilling" despite its nonsensical qualities from a scientific point of view.

THE FORMS OF MODERNIZATION

The looseness of all social systems everywhere becomes especially accentuated in the situation of "sponsored" modernization, and no single change-model is either possible on scientific grounds or likely to be followed by practical men of affairs. The rigidity of communist formulas is an ideological and political rigidity, not a scientific one, and other models for development are not only available in the abstract but also in the actual diversity of historical and contemporary developmental programs.

Modernization may start in a great variety of ways or in various aspects of a social structure, and may operate inconsistently in several of them simultaneously. Thus in colonial areas governed by a "pluralistic" metropolitan power, private schools sponsored by religious missionaries may turn out students with varying degrees of education for which there is in fact no effective use in the existing system of occupational recruitment. Or under the same political conditions the civil service, representing an official manifestation of colonial policy, may systematically recruit native employees on the basis of merit while private businessmen are permitted to follow a "color bar" principle in personnel policies.

Modernization in fact is not a strictly contemporary phenomenon.

Most of the underdeveloped areas of the world do not enter the era of feverish change since World War II as untouched traditional societies. The influence of Western European civilization on many other sectors of the globe is a matter of centuries, not decades. Even were there no intrinsic sources of dissidence, tension, and change—and we have established theoretical grounds for rejecting that simplifying assumption—the historical fact is that most underdeveloped areas enter the contemporary era with social systems already compounded of rather diverse cultural ingredients.

The process of modernization is most commonly approached in terms of "economic development." This has a high but not absolute validity, for it is possible to find situations in which the immediate and short-run priority is accorded to the state, the school, or the rural community. Yet rising per-capita levels of living have a kind of unquestioned value in developing areas, and economic development has a rather important instrumental value for most other "reforms" that may be ultimately justified on other grounds. A few examples are again in order.

The provision of a modern civil service may have intrinsic values in terms of simple administrative efficiency, the maintenance of order, and the preservation of the power of an existing political system. It is quite unlikely that corruption will be reduced, full-time and merit-selected personnel be chosen, or a kind of administrative ethic be established without a salary schedule that is virtually impossible in impoverished economies.

Education may be viewed as essential for an informed electorate in a democratic regime, or as an agency for political indoctrination in order to subvert the conservative influence of the family in revolutionary regimes, or as a form of cultural "consumer good" for states dedicated to cultivation of the "good life." But schools and books and teachers require money or its equivalent, and that means diverting resources from food or factories or firearms.

Land reform may be sought as a matter of social justice (or political support) and is likely to involve income redistribution rather than an increase in total income. In fact, almost all land reforms initially reduce aggregate output, and are likely to have their intended lasting effect only if new capital, improved techniques, and changed marketing procedures are also available to the newly independent rural cultivator.

It is reasonably proper, though conventional, therefore, to consider modernization in terms of economic growth. In fact, we may pursue the convention further and speak of the process as *industrialization*. Industrialization means the extensive use of inanimate sources of power for economic production, and all that that entails by way of organization, transportation, communication, and so on. Since many underdeveloped areas are now predominantly agricultural it is sometimes argued that industrialization in the sense of factory production of non-agricultural products is an improper model of economic growth for such areas. Yet very little increase in agricultural output is likely to be achieved without the use of industrial products, local or foreign—machines and chemical fertilizers, for example—and very little economic benefit is likely to accrue to an agricultural economy that does not have a local or foreign industrial market. Industrialization, then, includes mechanization of agriculture, and of the ancillary services of transportation and communication which are essential to the operation of a specialized and therefore interdependent economy.

The studies of social change that take industrialization as a starting point are extremely numerous, and naturally range widely in time, place, and degree of comparative generalization. Most of them suffer from a common defect, that of treating industrialization as a given change and recording or ordering of the consequential changes that must then follow, by pursuing the functional model of an integrated social system, which has to achieve a new basis of integration owing to the introduction of a critically important alteration in a strategic sector of society, the economy.

We have already attempted some fairly simple explanations of why industrialization is likely to be introduced into a contemporary society, but that is still not a completely satisfactory solution to the quest for a dynamic model. The connection between "before" and "after" in terms of sequences or processes of change would also be desirable, and for that desideratum the evidence is extremely poor. What is needed is not some invariant sequence according to some law of mindless evolution, for in fact real alternatives exist and real choices are made by real people. Yet varying sequences of change are evident, and all are not equally effective in achieving professed goals. And again, it is unlikely that there is "one best way" in view of the rather impressive variety of relevant conditions and of historic paths to the present evident in the areas now seeking or embarking on modernization.

In the present state of knowledge, the most impressive array of generalizations derive from before-and-after comparisons, which can be called the "comparative statics" of industrialization without meaning to derogate the established relationships. Here the model of the functionally integrated social system cuts with a double edge, though still leaving some questionable strands unsevered. The model informs us theoretically, and a multitude of observational studies confirm empirically, which elements of pre-industrial social systems cannot persist in an industrialized economy. The model also informs us theoretically, with empirical confirmation, concerning the new modes of social organization required by an industrial system. The strands that are missing, and must remain missing until the proper questions are properly put to data, include the range and temporal duration of tolerable variation, and particularly the sequential connections between primal cause—industrialization—and ultimate effect—a modernized society.

Although the solution is not ideal, there is some gain in distinguishing structural preconditions on the one hand and the concomitants and consequences of industrialization on the other. This is a first step toward the desirable "sequence models." It is the arrangement that we shall adopt here.

INDUSTRIALIZATION: CONDITIONS[1]

Economic development, universally sought as a matter of public policy and social welfare by the officials of underdeveloped and advanced countries alike, requires something more than the pious wish for a better life coupled with some simple tricks of technology and organization. In fact, this goal itself is a major precondition of economic development, for some industrialization may occur in the face of official indifference or hostility, but it is not likely to proceed very far very fast.

Values

This first component of the category—*values*—is in the contemporary world a kind of check-list point, though it was long and tediously disputed by scholars overly impressed with cultural diversity. The problem, we have noted, is not likely to arise at this level, but rather in the instrumental steps that touch on other, inconsistent value premises.[2] Values provide the rationale for particular norms, or rules of organization and conduct. The value of economic growth requires, for example, a fairly high degree of individual mobility and a placement system grounded on merit in performance, and that requirement is likely to come into conflict with a number of strongly supported values relating to the primacy of kinship position and obligations as a moral virtue. In this sense extensive value changes are the most fundamental condition for economic transformation. It would be improper to take a kind of pure or totalitarian view of this situation, however, for in effect it is quite unlikely that a system will be altered in such a "logical" fashion, even if a kind of theo-

---

1. This section is mainly based on Wilbert E. Moore, "The Social Framework of Economic Development," in Ralph Braibanti and Joseph J. Spengler (eds.), *Traditions, Values, and Socio-Economic Development* (Durham: Duke University Press, 1961), pp. 57–82. For a somewhat more elaborate scheme for analyzing "social aspects of economic development," see Moore, *The Impact of Industry* (Englewood Cliffs, N.J.: Prentice-Hall, 1965), in which conditions, first-order consequences, and reverberations are distinguished.

2. See the discussion by Feldman and Moore of "development as end and means" pp. 5–7 in their chapter "Commitment of the Industrial Labor Force," in Moore and Feldman (eds.), *Labor Commitment and Social Change in Developing Areas* (New York: Social Science Research Council, 1960).

retical model of necessary alterations is subscribed to by the agents of change. Rather, many necessary procedural or behavioral changes will be perceived in due course as inconsistent with pre-existent values, and the resulting tensions will constitute problems that will be only partially resolved by change in values.

There is another value, however, that is likely to be of temporal as well as logical significance. That is a high degree of national integration or, in short, *nationalism*. Although various economic transformations have occurred in the face of some political instability and in colonial areas, the rapid and deliberate change that forms the contemporary pattern of modernization has been associated with rather extreme nationalism. The association is scarcely accidental, since nationalism provides a kind of non-rational focus of identification and rationale for the extensive disruption of the traditional order. Germani, referring to this national identification and acceptance of the legitimacy of political authority as "mobilization," notes its general absence in Latin America as an impediment to economic development in countries rich in resources.[3]

Institutions

We next turn to *institutional* conditions for industrialization, meaning by institutions, complexes of norms relating to a major aspect of social structure—for example, marriage or economic exchange. Institutions are relational in social systems in a dual sense.

> 1. They furnish the codes that tie patterns of action and organization to social values.
> 2. They are to some degree interstitial between particular social structures, for in governing the behavior in a major context of action they also relate that context to others. Marriage, for example, constitutes a set of primary relevance to the family, but also provides a major link between the family and other segments of society.

Clearly the institutional conditions of industrialization we should look for first are predominantly economic. Here we may identify property, labor, and exchange.

The institution of *property* provides a normative definition of rights in scarce values. The essential condition for industrialization is that such rights be transferable, for new uses of land and other resources, raw materials and semi-finished products, and financial capital are entailed in mobilizing the "factors of production." Substantial restraints on property transfers impede or prevent such mobilization. The alternative of socialist

---

3. Gino Germani, "Démocratie Representative et Classes Populaires en Amérique Latine," *Sociologie du Travail* (October-December, 1961), 3:408–25.

ownership does not escape this institutional condition, for transfers must still be made between those who are administratively responsible for the various resources and materials.

Labor, too, must be mobile. Labor mobility entails not only the likelihood of geographical relocation but also, and more significantly, social relocation. In particular, for the complex array of tasks entailed in an industrial system, labor recruitment must be strongly based on performance qualifications without primary regard to prior social position.

An industrial order also requires a commercialized system of *exchange*. Even socialist states have not been able to avoid placing monetary values on resources and goods as they move through the productive system, and financial payments to all economic participants form the essential link between specialized producers and generalized consumers. The markets may not be "free," supplies and prices may be administratively determined, but distribution of goods and services in an industrial economy involves financial transactions nevertheless.

The counterpart of national integration as a value-condition for industrialization is a set of political codes and procedures that assure a large measure of political stability.[4] Industrialization in the narrow sense of factory production entails very expensive fixed capital installations that would be especially vulnerable to civil disorder. But other industrial requirements are perhaps even more important. The "factors of production" (raw materials, power, building and equipment, labor) rarely exist at a single place, and often must be moved over considerable distances. And orders and sales are rarely instantaneously completed. Most financial transactions must operate on credit. Thus agreements or contracts must be dependable, and if necessary enforceable. All this assumes *political stability* extensive in space and time. In the absence of fairly reliable legal principles and their judicial application, along with simple civil order, it is likely to be nearly impossible to establish or continue the complex economic network that industrialism implies.

There is still another institutional condition less clearly linked to major organizational segments of societies, although it has a fairly close relationship to schools at various levels and to whatever organizations, private or public, which serve to promote science and especially technology and the formulation of economic plans. This condition may be called, in a kind of shorthand, the *institutionalization of rationality*. The important point is that some leading sectors of the population must be committed not only to the ideal of economic growth but also to its practical implementation in terms of programs and plans, the identification

---

4.   See Colin Leys (ed.), *Politics and Change in Developing Countries* (Cambridge: Cambridge University Press, 1969), especially the essay by J. P. Nettl, "Strategies in the Study of Political Development," pp. 13–34.

of necessary techniques to be borrowed or adapted or even invented for unusual applications. A problem-solving orientation and dedication to deliberate change are rather general characteristics in fully industrial societies, but some degree of such orientation among governors and administrators is a condition for even getting started.[5] One principal historical focus for this kind of orientation was to be found in the role of the entrepreneur. In many contemporary developing areas, the equivalent of the entrepreneur is to be found in the government's central planning agencies, but these agencies must be seconded by a great variety of technicians.

Organization

Some of the *organizational* requirements for industrialization are obvious, some less so. Thus the technology of factory production must be linked with the techniques of specialization and coordination in the organization of work itself. This means concretely that some approximation to the model of the specialized and hierarchically governed *bureaucracy* or "administrative organization" is essential. Similarly, there must be some orderly structure for making decisions. In a pluralistic or "laissez-faire" system, decisions are made at the level of the individual firm, but still within a framework of governmental policies and market operations. In virtually all developing areas the desire for speed, if nothing else, prompts governmental leaders to take a strong lead in developmental plans, if not in outright administration.

An appropriate *fiscal organization of the state*, at least as banker and tax collector, is also necessary. And what is sometimes called "social overhead capital" in the form of transportation and communication constitutes a further set of organizational requirements. At the "house-keeping" level, the provision of housing, streets, water and sewers, and public transportation for the cities and towns that grow as a consequence of modernization may strain national resources simultaneously needed for more productive investment.

Motivation

A simple desire for a better life, then, does not automatically lead to its own fulfillment. Institutional and organizational changes intervene. And even *motivation* cannot be automatically assumed. Hagen

---

5. See the discussion of "creativity as a requisite," by Everett E. Hagen, *On the Theory of Social Change* (Homewood, Ill.: Dorsey, 1962), pp. 30–34. See also Douglas E. Ashford, "Attitudinal Change in Modernization," in Chandler Morse and others, *Modernization by Design* (Ithaca: Cornell University Press, 1969), pp. 147–85.

would put creativity or the innovative personality practically at the head of the list of conditions for development that cannot be assumed.[6] Although Weber's[7] emphasis on the importance of the "Protestant Ethic" as precedent to the emergence of capitalism is clearly not a necessary precondition of industrialization in the contemporary world, some degree of "achievement orientation," of ambition for personal betterment and the acquisition of the education and skills to further that ambition, must exist in some groups and spread rather widely, if sustained growth is to be accomplished.[8] Incidentally, it appears that a widespread sense of *participation* in changing the social order is a more felicitous condition for modernization than the simple requirement of passive adjustment by most of the population, and certainly more auspicious than apathy or hostile opposition.

These then are the major social prerequisites for industrializing an economy. To these we must add the more strictly economic conditions relating to capital formation, investment ratios in the various sectors of the economy, and the character of foreign assistance and foreign trade. In combination, they do not guarantee successful modernization, but absence of one or another condition will impede or prevent success.

How these changes are to be brought about in developing areas now must probably be given a different answer from that provided by their often slow development in the history of the industrialized Western World. Although no single instigating agency of deliberate change is likely to be absolutely sovereign, even in a totalitarian society, the state is likely to be more influential than any other social structure even in a pluralistic society. However much one may regret the increasingly *political* character of the contemporary world since this entails governmental expansion, the quest for modernization must almost certainly feature political mobilization as the major instrumentality of change.

INDUSTRIALIZATION: CONCOMITANTS AND CONSEQUENCES

To generalize across time and space concerning the changes in major aspects of societies that accompany industrialization involves the neglect of otherwise important differences. The diversity of societies

6. Ibid., especially Chap. II, "Emergence of Technological Creativity."

7. See Max Weber, *The Protestant Ethic and the Spirit of Capitalism*, trans. Talcott Parsons (New York: Scribner's, 1930).

8. Alex Inkeles conducted an extensive comparative analysis of the "modernization of man." For a brief summary, see his essay, "The Modernization of Man," in M. Weiner (ed.), *Modernization: The Dynamics of Growth* (New York: Basic Books, 1966), pp. 138–50.

prior to modernization is one source of difference, and the historical period in which industrialization occurs is another.

> In some situations history itself prevents its own repetition for its lessons and results become the basis of new social actions. The simplest illustration of this is the lack of necessity for a newly developing economy to repeat either the timing or sequence of technological change. More fundamentally, there now exist a number of advanced industrial economies, which, even if they are viewed as converging, still provide alternative models of ideology, political control, and peripheral or non-core structural features. The available models permit a degree of choice to the developing area that earlier innovators did not have.[9]

Despite these differences, and the effect they have in adding to the variety of rates and sequences of change, we may still go rather far in identifying the structural changes that are functionally associated with economic modernization.

In summarizing the great number of particular or comparative studies, it is convenient to take the organization of production as a condition, though it will of course continue to change as modernization proceeds. For example, the close machine-pacing of the factory worker may give way to a degree of machine "mastery" as more nearly automated plants become technologically and economically feasible. Likewise, as the educational and technical levels of the labor force increase, administrative direction is likely to become less autocratic as procedural decisions are made by those directly involved in one or another productive or administrative process.

Taking the organization of work as part of the "core structure" of industrialization, we may move out to other changes in economic structure, to changes in population size and composition (demographic structure), and changes in geographical distribution of population (ecological structure), and complete the tour by concentrating on characteristic aspects of social organization in the narrow sense. Because of the extremely wide range of our attention, an attempt will be made to reduce the complexities that would interest the specialized student of modernization and get at the main changes that can be formulated much as a set of propositions.

Economic Organization

With respect to the effect of industrialization on principal features of *economic organization*, the following generalizations apply:

9. Arnold S. Feldman and Wilbert E. Moore, "Industrialization and Industrialism: Convergence and Differentiation," *Transactions of the Fifth World Congress of Sociology*, Washington, September, 1962, 2:151–69, quotation, by permission of the International Sociological Association, p. 158.

FOR MANY AREAS OF THE WORLD, the first major transformation involves incorporating what we may call the subsistence sector into the commercialized market system of the national economy. Substantial portions of the agrarian populations in many of the underdeveloped areas of the world essentially exist apart from the balance of the society, self-sustaining at a meager level but neither producing surpluses for the rest of the economy nor providing a market for the products of industrial enterprise.

INDUSTRIALIZATION entails a substantial reduction in the proportion of population directly engaged in agriculture. (Even in prosperous "agricultural" economies such as Denmark and New Zealand, a minority of the economically active population actually draws its livelihood from farming.) The application of modern methods to agriculture reduces the direct labor demand for production while manufacturing and a variety of ancillary services claim new quotas of workers.

SOME SHORTAGE OF SKILLED WORKERS is an endemic condition in developing industrial societies, even though there may well be surpluses of unskilled workers or workers whose skills have become obsolescent with technical change.

THERE IS A LONG-TERM UPGRADING of minimum- and average-skill levels required in an industrial economy. The shape of the skill distribution changes from the "hour glass" to a triangle or pyramid, with the great majority of workers relatively unskilled because they could not be otherwise at new occupations, to a diamond-shaped structure with relatively few truly unskilled workers and the vast majority of workers in various "middle" categories. (See Fig. 17.)

AT FINER GRADES of occupational distinction, the demand for highly trained

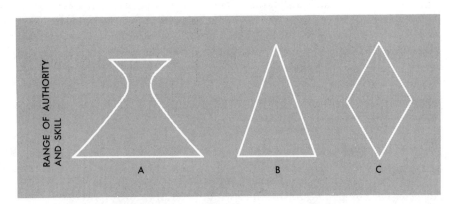

Figure 17. Distribution of industrial personnel by degree of authority and skill: **A.** Earliest stage of industrialization, **B.** "Transitional" or "early mature" stage of industrialization, **C.** "Advanced" industrialization.

professionals of all categories increases in the course of modernization. The early ascendancy of physicians and industrial engineers never completely disappears, but their relative position tends to diminish as newer professional types—particularly experts in organization and in various relations, ranging from law to the general public—gain in prominence.

THE MANNING OF THE OCCUPATIONAL STRUCTURE of an industrial society requires a high degree of labor mobility, both within individual careers and as between generations.

THE DIFFERENTIATION OF THE OCCUPATIONAL STRUCTURE only partly involves scalar differences in income, prestige, and security. Also involved is a tremendous lateral extension of occupations that imply various social differences but not a set of distinctions that can be represented by social strata.

WHATEVER THE METHOD of securing investment capital for initial modernization, continuous growth entails the reinvestment of profits either through the voluntary choice of investors or by the direct intervention of the state.

JUST AS THE "SUBSISTENCE SECTOR" of some underdeveloped areas must be brought within the national productive economy, industrialization requires the universal extension and commercialization of markets for consumer goods. Financial and commercial operations tend to expand in industrial economies, but in many underdeveloped areas such operations are already extensive though economically inefficient.

WITH RISING MINIMUM and average per-capita incomes, the consumption of "necessities" first rises, followed by various comforts and luxuries. Eventually, services represent a rising proportion of consumer expenditures as compared with all types of consumer goods. The range of goods, including both highly specialized items and alternative products for the same use, expands steadily with industrialization.

THOUGH MODES OF DISTRIBUTION vary widely, for example, as between socialist and liberal economies, all distribution systems share a complex interdependence among suppliers, retailers, and consumers; and although specialization of functions tends generally to increase economic productivity, it also makes interdependent systems especially vulnerable to any form of failure or interruption of performance.

Demographic and Ecological Structure

The changes to be expected in the *demographic and ecological structure* of societies in the course of industrialization yield another set of generalizations:

THE THEORY OF THE "DEMOGRAPHIC TRANSITION," discussed briefly in Chapter 2, states that the high mortality rates characteristic of underdeveloped areas will decline before fertility rates, which are also high. This condition leads to rapid "transitional" growth. Stated in these abstract terms, the generalization appears applicable to developing areas. However, demographic trends provide an especially clear case of the significance of differences in historical eras. In the older industrial countries reductions in mortality were chiefly the consequence of economic growth. Public health and medical techniques are now available to other countries, however, so that the downward course of death rates is likely to be faster, and to precede substantial changes in economic structure.

THE DIRE PREDICTIONS OF MALTHUS of increasing misery due to population growth were not confirmed in the West, partly because of expansion into thinly settled areas of the New World and Oceania, partly because population growth appears to have stimulated economic growth by providing manpower and consumer demand. The more rapid growth in developing areas, without the safety valve of emigration, already shows signs of depressing the growth of per-capita income.

THE MOTIVES for family limitation in the West, though different in particular ways from one country and time to another, are generally thought to be economic, including aspirations for mobility for self and for children. Similar motives are likely to be effective eventually as modernization reaches more deeply into the underdeveloped areas. Knowledge and availability of contraceptive techniques, though not as crucially significant as a motivational change, are still likely to be significant for the rate of change and the order in which various segments of the population shift to a small-family pattern. It is probable that the Western pattern of adoption of family limitation first by urban middle- and upper-income groups will be repeated in industrializing countries. At the very earliest stage of family limitation, the women practicing contraception are likely to have a higher fertility than the general average, as they will be women who already have "too many children." The planning of family size from the beginning is a somewhat later development.

MORTALITY REDUCTION commonly is not spread evenly across all ages, but rather affects most strongly infants and children. These reductions, with continuing high birth rates, yield "young" populations in terms of average age, and for developing areas add to the difficulty of extending educational facilities.

EXPANSION OF ECONOMIC OPPORTUNITIES also is likely to be very uneven in space. The historical association between industrialization and urbanization is by no means complete, but is very pronounced. Migration to new centers of employment redistributes population. Migrants are predominantly young adults, but whether they are "positively" or "negatively" selected in terms of education, intelligence, or various social qualities is not generally known, for effective studies of internal migration are few and scattered.

MOST OF THE UNDERDEVELOPED AREAS of the world are now experiencing "over-urbanization"—that is, migration from rural areas at a rate higher than the expansion of employment opportunities in the cities. The reasons for this phenomenon are largely speculative, but it appears to be massive testimony to the spread of economic discontent and the urgent quest for a better life.

MANY OF THESE URBAN IN-MIGRANTS eke out an existence in various marginal "service" occupations, thus producing a more rapid expansion of employment in services than in manufacturing, contrary to the developmental sequence in the older industrial countries.

THOUGH RAPID URBANIZATION tends to "distort" the investment patterns in developing areas, the expansion of urban slums and their inhabitants has a high "political visibility," which may have an effect on the urgency with which official measures to promote economic reform are undertaken.

Social Structure

The variety of political regimes and of other elements of social systems in advanced industrial societies warns against a too-rigid functional determinism related to economic modernization. The extent to which industrial societies have moved or are moving to a kind of common destination, discussed in the final section of this chapter, is clearly not so great that there are no differences from one time and place to another in the "social consequences" of industrialization. Nevertheless, economic modernization does have some invariant implications for *social structure* and imposes rather sharp limits on the variation of some other features of social organization:

THE EXTENSIVE MOBILITY, both geographical and social, appropriate to industrializing and industrial societies has negative consequences for extended kinship systems and tends to reduce the close ties between adult generations and adult siblings. Although some scholars have taken the view that only the small-family system is possible in industrial societies, this generalization is too sweeping. The social responsibilities to kinsmen beyond the "nuclear" family of parents and their immature children become weakened and permissive rather than obligatory, but may endure. "Corporate" kin groups, acting as economic and political entities, will not survive the impact of a modernizing economy, but remnants of reciprocity are likely to remain. Even the generalization concerning "corporate" kinship is subject to exceptions. It often survives, even in urban America, among the hereditary poor, and conspicuously among the hereditary rich.

EXTENSIVE "FAMILY DISORGANIZATION" is likely to accompany the breakdown of traditional patterns and the incomplete establishment of new institutions. This "transitional" disorganization is not the same as the disorganization arising from marital separations and divorces in industrial societies. Separation and divorce are likely to derive from the very intensity of interaction within the small family, which serves an almost unique emotional function in modern societies. Such instability cannot be taken as a sign of family decay through "loss of functions."

BOTH MATE SELECTION and parent-child relationships are affected by the "individualism" that modernization fosters, even in societies with a collectivist ideology. Marriage by arrangement between kin groups is virtually certain to disappear—this being one of the kinship bonds that is weakened or severed—and voluntary mate selection to appear in its stead. Children will receive some of their training at the hands of persons other than their parents, and some of that training will entail knowledge and skills that their parents do not share. Thus some tension between the generations, even before children leave their parental families, is virtually inevitable.

AS THE FAMILY HAS CEASED to be an economically productive unit, especially in the urban setting, the social position of women has changed. The initial impact of economic modernization may be viewed as actually reducing the status of women by increasing their economic dependence. Later, however, in highly modernized societies women benefit from increased employment opportunities and greater freedom of movement and of time-dispositions. Continued economic subordination may be challenged through political articulation of demands for equality. Even within fairly conventional families, women have assumed greater authority in two significant respects, in part because of the absence of males who are away at places of employment: the supervision of children, and the disposition of family income at least for ordinary consumption. In this connection, the usual statements to the effect that the family loses its economic functions with advancing industrialization is inaccurate, for the family is the usual consuming unit in a modern economy and thus the source of important economic decisions.

THE INDUSTRIAL COMMUNITY or city normally assembles persons of diverse social backgrounds, often from different tribes, countries, and "cultures." Especially in these circumstances "informal" social controls are likely to be radically weakened, and formal agencies for maintaining order required.

FOR SOME URBAN DWELLERS the loss of meaningful intimate bonds with others will produce various symptoms of apathy and alienation. Alcoholism, various mental disorders, and drug addiction may well increase in the course of rapid economic change and persist as various economic and social dislocations exact their toll on those who do not adapt well to the process.

THE NEED FOR LITERACY and for various levels of technical skills in the course of modernization leads to a great emphasis on schools and other agencies of education. For the country barely embarking on economic modernization, there is some dispute concerning the "correct" use of limited resources for education: the rapid production of a new technical and administrative elite, or the widest possible expansion of elementary education. In view of the nearly universal demand for education as a symbol of progress, political realities are likely to weight the balance toward broadening the educational base through primary schools.

MASS COMMUNICATION, particularly that made possible by the technology of radio transmission, may provide a partial substitute for widespread literacy as a basis of national political consciousness. This substitution, however, is relatively ineffective for the more technical uses of literacy in employment, marketing, and the like. The major effect of mass communication is likely to be that of breaking down village isolation rather than inculcating any particular set of political attitudes.

THE STANDARDIZATION OF "POPULAR CULTURE" through the media of mass communication is likely to be less extreme than some critics fear. Regional dialects persist in the most advanced industrial countries, for example, despite exposure to a common dialect through radio and television. Some traditional forms of recreation—"native" dances and fiestas, for example—may be adversely affected by "cultural" standardization, but not necessarily. Traditional practices not absolutely inconsistent with modernization may be deliberately supported as a mark of cultural identity and continuity, and perhaps as a tourist attraction.

INDUSTRIALIZATION INTRODUCES a relatively sharp division between "work" and "leisure," a distinction either missing or vague in a tribal or agrarian society. Time-dispositions of all sorts are affected by this division, and leisure may become a problem for some sectors of the population, and particularly for those whose jobs hold little intrinsic interest.

MODERNIZATION BRINGS IN ITS WAKE a proliferation of interest groups and associations, representing not only occupational or other economic interests and divisions but also various common interests in hobbies such as collecting postage stamps or antique furniture, in appreciation of the arts, or in forms of physical recreation. Even where the social structure is highly "politicized" in totalitarian states, distinct groups form around specialized social functions or individual preferences.

PARTICIPATION IN ASSOCIATIONS, at least where it is voluntary, tends to be unequally distributed in the population, and to be highest among those who are also in responsible or creative positions in occupations or other "fundamental" activities.

SECULAR ATTITUDES ARE ENCOURAGED by the "institutionalization of rationality", but rational orientations are not wholly satisfactory in handling all of life's problems—for example, personal misfortune and bereavement. Some form of religious orientation exhibits a hardy power of survival even in societies where secularization has been adopted as an official ideology. One form or another of national patriotism may provide partial, but only partial, substitutes for more traditional systems of religious belief.

THE MODES OF SOCIAL DIFFERENTIATION and the unequal allocation of social status and rewards to various positions and functions are affected in major degree by industrialization. In general it is proper to say that a society undergoing modernization will exhibit competing systems of social stratification. Within the modernized social sector, the early impact of new occupations and positions tends to establish a polarization between the innovating and directing elements on the one hand and the relatively unskilled and reluctant participants on the other. (Refer back to Fig. 17.)

This polarization, contrary to Marx, diminishes through time as great varieties of "intermediate" positions are created, and as "lateral" differentiation is added to simple differences along a single scale.

INCOME DIFFERENCES take on a special significance in industrialized societies for two reasons. First, income is the medium for allocating not only the economy's consumption goods but also a growing number of services that may have been rendered on non-market bases in traditional societies. Second, income tends to be the major way of reliably ranking people on a uniform scale, but it has a variable and often a low or no relationship to other bases of social differentiation. For both individuals and groups the multitude of contexts in which status is relatively independent of income and from other contexts gives rise to widespread "status inconsistency," that is, reduces the significance of the notion of a "global" social status.

FINALLY, WE HAVE SEEN that the *political* structure of the state is not closely determined by industrialization. It is, however, virtually certain that the widespread tensions and dislocations accompanying rapid social transformation will receive political attention, and that some form of extensive political participation by the general public will be necessary for any regime able to continue in political control. That participation may be highly controlled and manipulated rather than voluntary and democratic, but it is very likely to appear in some form. At the same time, the combined importance of nationalism and of maintaining a modicum of political control in parlous times makes its likely that a military establishment will be a prominent feature of modernizing states.

THE OUTCOME OF MODERNIZATION is considerably narrower with regard to the *administrative* structure of the state. Here one may expect to see developing various approximations to the model of the "rational" bureaucracy," which is finally accountable politically, but which relies on technical division of labor and coordination by delegated, impersonal authority to carry out the multitude of functions that the modern operation of the national state entails.

We have completed a rather long journey through the "social consequences of industrialization," though other stopovers and side trips might have been made here and there on the way. But the journey in a sense has no end, for there is no clear and precise point at which an "industrializing" society becomes an "industrial" one. The distinction, though conventional, is rather arbitrary, and we can continue our discussion directly to the continuing changes in industrial societies.

THE DYNAMICS OF INDUSTRIAL SOCIETIES

Modern industrial societies are continuously dynamic, and indeed appear to change at a steadily accelerating rate. The crude experiences of everyday life, the things that "everyone knows," confirm the changeful qualities of social structure and patterns of behavior more nearly than do the expert treatises of sociologists, and this requires some comment supplementary to our discussion in Chapter 1 of the "static models" in customary use in sociological theory.

Contemporary sociological writing is by no means lacking in discussions of structural changes, but by far the largest volume of descriptive and analytical work on social dynamics relates to particular (though very complex) processes of transformation that we have just reviewed: the modernization of non-literate or other traditional societies.

> The essential character of the assumptions underlying most of the discussion of industrialization may be summarized by three interrelated but analytically separable positions.
>
> 1. Economic transformation is viewed as the intermediate phase of a three-stage model of social transformation: (a) a static, pre-industrial stage, (b) a dynamic transitional stage, and (c) a static stage following the "industrial revolution."
>
> 2. During transition, industrialism is viewed as an externally induced system that has a problematic impact on the presumably static and resistant traditional structure. Structural analysis is used to trace through the consequences of the new set of social elements, but only rarely is attention given to the interaction of structures in juxtaposition, and the resulting modification of the structure of industrialism.
>
> 3. Although antecedent cultures are conceded to be widely diverse, the process of industrialization is viewed as leading to a common destination. When the transition is complete, the required structural changes in social systems will have been made, the boxes will be "filled in," and the post-industrial societies, implicitly static, are explicitly alike.[10]

Each of these assumptions can be challenged. The one of immediate interest is that full industrialization ends the dynamic processes associated with the transition to that stage. Once stated baldly, it becomes ridiculous, and could only have arisen out of a peculiar division of scholarly labor whereby students of modern societies have concentrated their attention on the interdependence of structures, leaving to students of industrialization a concern for change.

Restoration of Traditional Patterns

One of the relatively small-scale but significant changes characteristic of industrial societies is the way in which the rather sharp breaks with the past attendant on early industrialization may end up being temporary or partial. The restoration of a complete *status quo ante* is improbable in any sector of social life, for too many interdependent

---

10. Feldman and Moore, "Industrialization and Industrialism," pp. 152–53.

changes have meanwhile occurred. Partial reconstruction may occur, however.

Let us take kinship and family organization as an example. Strong emphasis on the bonds of lineage, the *consanguine* principle of familial organization, is clearly inconsistent with individual mobility on merit. The separation of small family units, and especially the probability that young adults will seek new employments in new locations as industrialization proceeds, provide both a spatial and a social foundation for the appearance of the *conjugal* family with its emphasis on the marital unit and its immature children. The different generations and perhaps even adult siblings are likely to represent and be intimately involved in quite radically different social settings and styles of life. But as most of the society becomes modernized, those differences diminish or disappear. Meanwhile, improved transportation and communication reduce the significance of distance, and communication and visiting become fairly easy.

In any event, it is asking a great deal—nearly the impossible—of human motivation for persons involved for years in the intimate associations of the small family to treat one another as strangers after children have married and established their own households. It was suggested in Chapter 4 that consanguine and conjugal principles of familial organization are not mutually exclusive but rather are always competitive. The considerations just advanced indicate that the predominant emphasis on conjugal principles with early industrialization subsequently diminishes somewhat, and kinship claims that have never completely disappeared reassert themselves.

But what are these claims? Certainly not that all small-family units will fare equally. Rather that kinsmen become a first resort in adversity, including especially bereavement but not excluding financial difficulties. Generally, these become moral but optional obligations rather than mandatory ones, but that does not dismiss their operation.

It appears in effect that particularly in the United States, where the de-emphasis on lineage was perhaps the most extreme, extended kinship ties can now survive the social inequality of the distinct family units. This occurs in part by a degree of differentiation that makes exact comparison difficult, in part by simply avoiding the issue where comparison is easier, as with apparent income.

At the same time that public educational policies, for example, continue to reduce the inherited inequality of opportunity through the operation of the family as a socializing and status-placement agency for children, other tendencies are bolstering or at least restoring the emotional bonds of kinship.

Another example of partial restoration may be found in market behavior. The ideal of the impersonal market, with highly fractional relations among transacting partners, may operate in purer form where participants are literally strangers than in more enduring business relationships. The participant in a primitive market, with all its ancillary social functions, may have her counterpart in the suburban housewife who meets her friends at the supermarket. Similarly, a great deal of the financial operations in a relatively stable economy are likely to operate on trust rather than on detailed and impersonal contracts. But this, in turn, entails widespread acceptance of the norms of the modern economic system, an assumption that cannot be made as the new forms of enterprise and exchange have yet to establish their own conventions and traditions.

It would not do to exaggerate these partial restorations, for the social transformations involved in modernization run wide and deep. Yet where they do occur they are worthy of special note, for they are likely to reveal some of the enduring qualities of social systems generally that not even an industrial revolution can totally eradicate.

Processes of Continuous Change

A number of processes associated with advanced societies seem never to reverse direction. Outstanding among these is *specialization* in all its manifestations. Specialization takes the form of both individual role differentiation and the organization of collectivities around highly particularized functions. The two of course often go together, for a very specialized cooperative mission (say, eliminating water pollution coming from a manufacturing process) provides the basis for determining the combination of refined skills needed for its fulfillment (chemists, biologists, engineers, business economists or accountants, and probably trained inspectors to insure compliance with new standards adopted).

Although specialization is often regarded as a "given," a kind of natural law that requires no further explanation, it is important to seek its basis if it can be found. If we examine one of its most common manifestations, extreme subdivision of tasks in industrial production, the process seems primarily related to another source of change, the purposeful attention to productive technology. Yet even in this instance important social techniques are probably of greater significance. Specialization of this sort requires criteria of selection, communication, and administrative coordination of a rather high order. The circumstances are not radically different in other contexts, for coordination of some form is always the counterpart of specialization in a system that has any enduring qualities and is successful in its formal mission.

Size clearly encourages or at least makes possible specialization, and size again involves important elements of communication. Yet the interplay should also be noted. Specialization may also encourage growth of organized units by making possible rather elaborate relations through time and space.

Role differentiation often takes extreme forms even where it is not conspicuous. Feldman[11] has remarked that administrative statuses in membership units such as bureaucracies can be viewed as a constellation of positions in different and not entirely congruent analytical systems—for example, in a skill distribution, a system of authority, a communication network, a system of reward distribution, and a labor market. Nominally unitary positions thus are actually "fragmented," and the organizations of which they are a part are pervaded by partially alien systems.

One crude index of specialization, the number of distinguishable occupations, continues to grow in all industrial societies. New products and new processes do not uniformly displace old ones, and new services link specialists in new ways. Although some specialties may finally disappear and some differentiated tasks may be reassembled as a more complex occupation, the overwhelming trend toward greater differentiation continues.

Yet if we look to other aspects of social action, and particularly in the field of consumption standards and so-called "popular culture," social commentators emphasize growing homogeneity. The view is not undisputed, however, and in fact both positions are correct. The extremes of basic consumption standards do tend to narrow with growing prosperity, and conspicuously underprivileged groups may become more nearly assimilated to conventional standards. Yet prosperity also entails some measure of discretionary income, which by definition can be spent in diverse ways and even for what appears to be noncompeting goods and services. The very mass production that yields uniformity in some goods also yields the possibility of substantial variability in the combinations that particular consuming units may choose to put together.

Another sort of mixed process is to be found in the individual's immediate contexts of linkage to the great society. On the one hand we observe more numerous and more specialized interest groups, often putting the individual in the situation where he cannot protect his own interests and remain "unorganized." On the other hand, and contrary to the tendentious arguments about "loss of family functions," we find evidence of a revival of "familism" as about the only institutionally sanctioned organization where the individual may be treated as something like a whole person and legitimately display some emotion. The demands of jobs and of interest groups have not left the family unaffected, for

---

11. Arnold S. Feldman, "The Interpenetration of Firm and Society," in International Social Science Council, *Social Implications of Technological Change*, Paris, 1962, pp. 179–98.

there is a genuine competition for scarce time and energy. Yet it strongly appears that this leads precisely to a strengthening of the affective companionship functions of the family, not their weakening. Although the contemporary "commune" appears to be an attempt to serve functions similar to those of the family but on a more extensive basis, their relations with larger society are extremely precarious and few are truly self-subsistent and thus capable of continuing to exist apart from society.

The nature of social problems has a changeful character. This is true not only in the sense that new activities require new regulations and new ways of dealing with infractions, but also on the broader basis of the quality of discontent. Differences in the nature of work and the uses of leisure, the modes of obtaining a redress of grievances in a vastly complex political system, the arguments over general and specialized education, the preservation of local initiative in the face of centralized administrative controls—these are some of the problems that besiege modern industrial societies but did not do so in the same degree in the past. Since simple solutions are not evident, these tensions are likely to persist into the foreseeable future, and to be joined by others.

Organization of Change

On a previous occasion we noticed that an emphasis on rational problem solving in social affairs leads to deliberate innovation. A characteristic that advanced industrial societies share with those seeking to join that club, but not with most historic or primitive societies, is the high proportion of all changes that are either deliberate and planned or the secondary consequences of such changes. This characteristic is true in science and technology but also in legislation, the activities of "reform" and other interest groups, and in the development of strategies for situations ranging from petty market transactions to the conduct of international relations.

In major areas of social life change has become *organized* and *institutionalized*. The degree to which it is also centralized, the product and implementation of a "master plan," is of course quite variable. The extremes of totalitarian controls in communist countries and pluralistic decentralization in the Western democracies are clearly far apart. Yet the contrast is not total. Whether for reasons of domestic integration or especially for reasons of foreign policy, some centralized and coordinated planning exists at least in the larger democratic nations. On the other hand the communist countries permit some "liberty by default," some essentially private planning and manipulation of the environment, partly because the administrative costs of imposing complete controls on a complex system, even were it possible to do so, are likely to exceed the additional benefits.

Social planning varies not only in the *extent* of significant changes for which prediction and control may be sought (and thus in the degree of centralization), but also in the *temporal horizon*—the future that matters.[12] Relatively short planning horizons have been typical of public agencies and private businesses alike, mainly because of current accountabilities. Sacrifices or restraints in behalf of "posterity" are institutionalized mainly in terms of inheritance of wealth in family lineages, though protection of future natural resources (including space and the "natural" environment) is a matter of growing concern. Man's vaunted mastery of the environment turns out once more to be only partial, since mastery entails powers of destruction difficult or impossible to reverse.[13]

Planning clearly involves dealing with sequential systems and not simply interdependent ones.[14] And sequential systems entail in turn the capacity to predict secondary, tertiary, and nth-order consequences of current states or proposed interventions. Thus the discovery of long-term harmful effects of chemical pesticides used in agricultural production or the environmental damage from strip-mining has prompted lengthening horizons for so-called cost-benefit analyses and "technology assessment."

The concern for predicting future social problems and for measuring the effects of various deliberate interventions in shaping social policy has been the principal impetus for widespread interest in *social indicators*.[15] Indicators may be used as an "early warning" device, as a simplifying measure of current state (comparable to various economic indicators including Gross National Product) or as a measurement of past trends that are subject to extrapolation or projection into the future. This is not to say that there is no scientific interest in the measurement of social change and in moving from merely correlational to genuinely causal analysis. We are merely emphasizing the prominence of practical concerns, and those concerns are themselves of importance in appraising the significance of deliberate change in social systems. Since planning, even if extensive and centralized, is likely to be only partially effective,

12. See Alfred J. Kahn, *Theory and Practice of Social Planning* (New York: Russell Sage Foundation, 1969).

13. See Wilbert E. Moore, "Introduction" in Moore (ed.), *Technology and Social Change* (Chicago: Quadrangle Books, 1972).

14. See Wilbert E. Moore, "Toward a System of Sequences," in John C. McKinney and Edward A. Tiryakian (eds.), *Theoretical Sociology* (New York: Appleton-Century-Crofts, 1970), pp. 155–66; Walter Buckley, *Sociology and Modern Systems Theory* (Englewood Cliffs, N.J.: Prentice-Hall, 1967).

15. See Raymond A. Bauer (ed.), *Social Indicators* (Cambridge: M.I.T. Press, 1966); Eleanor Bernert Sheldon and Wilbert E. Moore (eds.), *Indicators of Social Change* (New York: Russell Sage Foundation, 1968).

various "mindless" models of changing systems have some partial validity. But "images of the future"[16] do make a difference in current and future social circumstances, and thus must be taken into account in attempts to predict the course of events.

Convergence and Divergence among Industrial Societies

The common structural features of industrial societies are undeniable and extensive. They form the solid factual basis for the generalizations we presented earlier concerning the conditions, concomitants, and consequences of industrialization. Yet short of the imposed order of a single world society—and even that would seem to require many federalistic elements and variations—it would be unsound to predict that social structures among industrial societies, present and future, will converge to the point of homogeneity.

Our earlier inability to generalize about the *political* structure of the industrial state takes on added significance in the context of comparing the future course of modern societies—if they indeed succeed in avoiding mutual destruction. The *major* ways in which industrial societies differ, and by all evidence and inference will continue to differ, are in their characteristic tensions and the ways these tensions are "managed," especially in a political context.

Let us go back to the industrialization process to find the principal, enduring sources of difference.[17]

THE COMMON STRUCTURAL REQUIREMENTS of industrialism mean that some antecedent structures cannot persist, and until they are changed they constitute barriers or impediments. But they are quite unlikely to be destroyed totally and without trace. In particular, the manner of their removal, the way the problem was solved, will almost certainly have enduring consequences.

VARIOUS ASPECTS of what may be called the "trajectory" of change also

---

16.   See Wendell Bell and James A. Mau (eds.), *The Sociology of the Future* (New York: Russell Sage Foundation, 1971); Wilbert E. Moore, "The Utility of Utopias," in Moore, *Order and Change* (New York: Wiley, 1967), pp. 292–304.

17.   A closely related and independently developed analysis is presented in Germani's essay "Démocratie Representative et Classes Populaires en Amérique Latine." See also Egbert de Vries, *Man in Rapid Social Change* (Garden City, N.Y.: Doubleday, 1961). Convergence theory is extensively argued by Marion J. Levy, Jr., *Modernization and the Structure of Societies* (Princeton: Princeton University Press, 1966), 2 vols. For an extension of the argument in the text, see Wilbert E. Moore, "The Singular and the Plural: The Social Significance of Industrialism Reconsidered," in Nancy Hammond (ed.), *Social Science and the New Societies* (East Lansing: Michigan State University, 1973), pp. 117–30.

produce differences in enduring social tensions. These include differences in sequence and timing of structural changes, in the rate of industrialization, in the historical era in which "modernization" begins.

ALTHOUGH THE OLDER INDUSTRIAL ECONOMIES by no means developed completely independently, contemporary developing areas can in a sense avail themselves of combinations of technology and social forms from a single world system, politically disordered though that system is.

WITH REGARD TO SOCIETIES now industrializing, the notion of convergence derives in part from the fundamental theoretical error that assumes industrialism to be a stable destination. Although developing areas are changing, so are "developed" ones.

WITH REGARD TO SOCIETIES now characterized as advanced or developed, there remain marked differences in political regimes, and there is no basis for assuming that the future will bring greater similarity, except possibly, and paradoxically, in details.

It is one thing to say that industrial societies share a range of principal structural features, and quite another, and a grossly improper thing, to say that the relative importance of those structures in society as a whole is the same or that the kinds of strain and linkage among them are the same. It is all very well to note that the Soviet factory manager resembles his American counterpart, but it does not follow that the structure of power and responsibility and the political environment of decision are similar. They are not, and no strong or even vagrant breeze now blowing is likely to make them so.

CHAPTER 6
SOCIAL EVOLUTION

The downfall of theories of social evolution, theories that were very popular late in the last century and a little beyond, came about in large measure from a paradoxical circumstance, the problem of diversity. Either the geographical, and thus cultural, scope was radically limited (usually the "classical" and historic civilizations of the Near Eastern and Western world) and the theories fell before new knowledge about Oriental and non-literate societies; or the diversity of cultures was made central to the evolutionary scheme, but the attempt to order differences by resorting to "stages" fell under both theoretical and empirical attack.

Since the first shortcoming was a relatively simple example of over-generalization, we need not dwell on it. The second shortcoming is somewhat more interesting and requires comment. The attempt to deal not only with historical sequences, which at least had a chronological order if not a clearly established evolutionary pattern, but also with comparative, contemporary societies raised a crucial theoretical problem. If, at a given time, societies were unequally evolved according to whatever criterion was being used, how would one account for these differences? Biological evolution, from which the leading ideas of social evolution were drawn, provided somewhat unsatisfactory answers. The notion of "adaptation" to differing environments offered some hope of accounting for cultural differentiation, but that required in turn a classification of environments and some attention to two additional problems: the connection between the setting and the social organization, and an explanation for the observed differences between "backwardness" and "advancement." One way of accounting for differences in evolutionary rates was to retain a biological interpretation by positing inequalities in "racial intelligence." Such explanations in turn came under attack for lack of direct evidence, and because any of the standard "racial" categories could be shown to have produced rather differing (and perhaps unequally "evolved") social systems.

Evolutionary scales were also subject to question from a somewhat different, more empirical source. The easy assumption that societies evolved from "simple" to "complex" forms, and that a scale based, say, on the predominant productive technology would order all significant aspects of social organization, turned out to be unwarranted. Durkheim, for example, in seeking the "most elementary" form of religion, reasoned that he would find it in a culture that had the simplest possible technology. From the comparative evidence available to him, he identified the "primitive" inhabitants of Australia as the simplest society known, and he proceeded to develop his theory of religion as a representation of society itself from that basis.[1] Although the theory does not precisely stand or fall on his mode of selection of a case for study, that case turned out to be very instructive in a negative way. As later demonstrated, for example by Warner,[2] the same aboriginal Australians that survived by simple hunting and food-gathering had an extremely complex kinship system, and in fact rather elaborate arrangements for observing ceremonial occasions.

The combined difficulties of squaring comparative evidence with "Western" history, of accounting for cultural differences in purely adaptive terms, and of finding a sure index of position on an evolutionary scale led to a rather radical "relativism" in social description. Not only did history become particularized for each society or closely related group of societies, but history itself tended to be minimized partly for want of facts concerning events that had occurred in the past in societies that were without written records.

The doctrine of "cultural relativity" inhibited even "static" or cross-sectional generalizations, until such developments as the "functional requisites of any society"[3] provided anew the basis for specifying the common features of societies. We have also been at some pains in this book to identify both general and typological characteristics of change in social systems. But what of social evolution, the broadly sequential fate of mankind generally?

---

1. Emile Durkheim, *The Elementary Forms of the Religious Life* (New York: Macmillan, 1915).

2. W. Lloyd Warner, *A Black Civilization* (New York: Harper, 1937).

3. See Marion J. Levy, Jr., *The Structure of Society* (Princeton: Princeton University Press, 1952), Chap. 4, "The Functional Requisites of Any Society."

The survival, or revival, of interest in social evolution has taken two principal forms. The one, exemplified in the work of Steward,[4] attempts to account for *diversity* by the concept of "multilineal evolution," which essentially means identification of different sequential patterns for different cultures, or types of cultures. This position remains more "programmatic" than propositional, and it is not clear from the program so far just what value the idea of evolution has for accounting for discrete patterns of change.

The other principal emphasis in the contemporary writing on social evolution is represented in the works of White[5] and of Sahlins and Service.[6] To these scholars the utility of a theory of social evolution is to be found at a *very* general level, and without insisting that all structural variations and dynamic processes be subsumed under or derivable from the general theory. To White,[7] especially, particular "cultures" are not the proper unit for study of cultural evolution, but culture in general. Although this approach begs the question of differentiation among social systems, including their unequal "evolution" at any particular time and by any test of relative position, it does serve to emphasize some common elements in the fate of mankind as a distinct biological species.

White has been appropriately criticized by Dobzhansky for exaggerating the discontinuity between biological and cultural evolution.[8] Dobzhansky correctly points to biological evolution as the necessary precondition for man's culture-creating capacity, and sees no reason to consider human heredity as thereafter irrelevant to that same capacity. He does of course agree that once man starts creating his own environment he may change his behavior far more rapidly than biological mutation and adaptation could occur. He also notes that the human environment becomes itself a major part of the biological process of adaptation. Yet he is quite correct in pointing out that social scientists tend to exaggerate the ascendancy of the social over the biological nature of man, while also noting the tendency of some human geneticists to exaggerate the possibilities of producing a "superior breed" under the assumption that there is a single set of ideal biological qualities to be selected. Man is clearly biologically differentiated as well as culturally differentiated.

4. Julian L. Steward, "Evolution and Social Typology," in Sol Tax (ed.), *Evolution After Darwin*, Vol. 2 (Chicago: University of Chicago Press, 1960), pp. 169–86.

5. Leslie White, *The Science of Culture* (New York: Grove Press, 1949).

6. M. D. Sahlins and E. R. Service, *Evolution and Culture* (Ann Arbor: University of Michigan Press, 1960).

7. White, *The Science of Culture.*

8. Theodosius Dobzhansky, *Mankind Evolving* (New Haven: Yale University Press, 1962).

The more fundamental difficulty in White's position is his exclusive emphasis on one index of man's social evolution, one agency by which man "progresses." This index, or agency, to White,[9] is the efficiency of power utilization. This contains part of the essential point, but only part. The more general proposition would maintain that there has been a long-term increase in man's ability to adapt to and control his environment, including, possibly, his "own" or the social environment in this proposition. Thus Boulding[10] notes the universality in human social organization of the "threat system," the "exchange system," and the "integrative system," which he subsumes under the *learning process* as the critical feature of social evolution.

Several extremely long-term trends are consistent with the thesis just stated:

FROM A FEW NOMADIC HUNTERS, the species *homo sapiens* has grown tremendously in numbers, in competition with other species for "life space." Although over shorter periods of time (which still may have been a matter of centuries) man's numbers have no doubt fluctuated, both survival and expansion bespeak an increasingly effective adaptation.

CLEARLY ONE OF THE MAJOR FACTORS in man's successful biological survival has been the additive or accumulative character of objective knowledge and rational technique.

YET THIS CUMULATED "SCIENCE" has been directed not only to man's material needs and comforts but also to a host of other concerns and interests, and not least to matters of social organization and social control. The invention of writing clearly accelerated the rate at which knowledge could be cumulatively stored and retrieved, just as that and other forms of communication-at-a-distance have broadened the span of social relations and lengthened the time during which knowledge may survive.

THE SIZE OF HUMAN POPULATIONS, the organized differentiation that size and communication and techniques of control make possible, lead to a further long-term trend. That is the increasing degree to which virtually all members of the species are part of a *single* system.[11] To view the contemporary world as unified seems to fly in the face of reason, since tremendous differentiation and sharp discords are patently evident. Yet, as we

9. White, *The Science of Culture.*

10. Kenneth E. Boulding, *A Primer on Social Dynamics* (New York: Free Press, 1970), Chap. 2, "Organizers of Social Evolution." See also Talcott Parsons, *Societies: Evolutionary and Comparative Perspective* (Englewood Cliffs, N.J.: Prentice-Hall, 1966).

11. See Wilbert E. Moore, *Order and Change* (New York: Wiley, 1967), Chap. 15, "Global Sociology: The World as a Singular System."

had occasion to remark in the preceding chapter, there exist common value orientations despite a multitude of differences in other values and in preferred forms of social relations, and there is an important sense in which both ideas and techniques are increasingly drawn from an international or intercultural pool to which many systems have contributed and more may do so in the future.

It may remain true for some time to come that many change sequences will be most readily studied in terms of societies or even less comprehensive systems. Such studies are likely to owe little to notions of social evolution for their intellectual grounding. Chance variation and selective adaptation may occur on a small scale, too, but often social change is also purposeful and rapid and the slower processes of evolution difficult to detect over the short run.

The longer term, however, is not an intellectually trivial preoccupation. The grand intellectual sweep of Spencer's philosophy,[12] which linked inorganic, organic, and superorganic (social) evolution, tended to be lost in the reaction to overgeneralization and in the special concerns of different scientific disciplines. Yet modern astrophysics, and particularly the works of scientifically oriented cosmologists, have made authoritative the conception of an "evolving universe."[13] And these intellectual preoccupations include speculations not only on the existence of intelligent life on other stars but also sobering speculations on a subject of rather critical interest to mundane man: Can an intelligent species that has achieved the reliable capacity for its own destruction avoid using it?

The uncertain answer to this question is usually given in terms of the necessity of social organization "catching up" with physical science, but that way of putting the matter poses a counterfeit dichotomy. Physical science is largely a product of social organization. The question is rather one of consistency or tolerable congruence within man's social arrangements. A retrospective view of man's history, if kept at a sufficiently general level, may well lead to fairly optimistic conclusions. A more nearly contemporary view, and particularly one that correctly attends to the way man has vastly speeded up the evolutionary clock, introduces a great element of caution if not outright pessimism. Man's social ingenuity, so barely won over so long a time and still so incomplete, has not yet demonstrated a clear capacity for resolving the very dangers that social evolution has itself produced.

12.   Herbert Spencer, *First Principles* (New York: Appleton, 1890).

13.   See, for example, George Gamow, "The Evolutionary Universe," *Scientific American*, September, 1956, 195:137–54.

SELECTED
REFERENCES

The works listed here are by no means all-embracing. They are intended primarily to acquaint the reader with some of the outstanding works in the field of social change and to stimulate further reading.

Robert A. Nisbet (ed.) *Social Change* (Oxford: Oxford University Press, 1972) provides a relatively brief and well-selected sampling of scholarly writing on social change. The same author's *Social Change and History* (New York: Oxford University Press, 1969) reviews the use of metaphors such as the life-cycle in grand theories of change and concludes with a perhaps too pessimistic view of large-scale theories. Kenneth E. Boulding, literate and witty as usual, combines the perspectives of the economist and the sociologist in *A Primer on Social Dynamics: History as Dialectics and Development* (New York: Free Press, 1970). Boulding's use of the term "primer" is an unduly modest description of a sophisticated (and highly readable) discussion.

Egbert De Vries, *Man in Rapid Social Change* (Garden City, N.Y.: Doubleday for World Council of Churches, 1961) is a relatively brief but well-organized discussion of the range of social changes, particularly in the context of economic modernization. The religious sponsorship of the book results in a policy discussion here and there, always clearly identified. A somewhat advanced general text that has achieved a reputation as a substantial scholarly source is R. M. MacIver and Charles H. Page, *Society* (New York: Rinehart, 1949). Not the least of its virtues is the extensive discussion of social change in Book III (Chaps. 22–29). In a relatively short book, *Man, Time, and Society* (New York: Wiley, 1963), Wilbert E. Moore considers time as a boundary condition for social systems and also as the measure of coordination and sequence. The temporal sequence of events is of critical importance in any attempt to analyze change.

Pitirim Sorokin, *Social and Cultural Dynamics*, one-volume ed. (Boston: Porter Sargent, 1957) is an abridgement made by the author of the famous four-volume work (New York: American Book, 1937–1940). Sorokin deals with temporal "fluctuations" among three predominant cultural systems and, more briefly, with structural changes. Theodosius Dobzhansky, an outstanding expert on human evolution, links biological and social evolution in a very sophisticated way in his *Mankind Evolving* (New Haven: Yale University Press, 1962). He notes how man's self-made environment becomes significant for his continuing physiological transformation. In *Evolution and Culture* (Ann Arbor: University of Michigan Press, 1960), M. D. Sahlins and E. R. Service present, and represent, the contemporary rediscovery of social evolution as a valuable frame of reference for dealing with long-term changes in the human condition. A much briefer analysis of modernization is that of Wilbert E. Moore, *The Impact of Industry* (Englewood Cliffs, N.J.: Prentice-Hall, 1965). Moore outlines the social conditions, concomitants, and consequences of industrialization. A somewhat more advanced (and necessarily less integrated) analysis of modernization is provided by a number of outstanding social scientists in a symposium: Nancy Hammond (ed.), *Social Science and the New Societies: Problems in Cross-Cultural Research and Theory Building* (East Lansing: Social Science Research Bureau, Michigan State University, 1973).

Bert F. Hoselitz and Wilbert E. Moore (eds.), *Industrialization and Society* (Paris and The Hague: UNESCO and Mouton, 1963) is an extensive volume which represents an excellent and comprehensive coverage of modernization, particularly the social concomitants and consequences of economic development. The hardy survival of Marxist interpretations of large-scale structural change may prompt some readers to consult the sources for this intellectual tradition. That task has been made much easier with the publication of an intelligently selected "reader": Robert C. Tucker (ed.), *The Marx-Engles Reader* (New York: Norton, 1972).

Although the principal title, *On the Theory of Social Change: How Economic Growth Begins* (Homewood, Ill.: Dorsey, 1962) is misleading, Everett E. Hagen does present a theory to account for the beginnings of rapid, economic development. The theory unites sociological and psychological approaches and makes the prime mover of change motivational. Descriptive materials from widely different societies are presented and interpreted from this point of view.

The problem of labor supply, labor performance, and acceptance by labor of the norms appropriate to an industrial society form the central focus of Wilbert E. Moore and Arnold S. Feldman (eds.), *Labor Commitment and Social Change in Developing Areas* (New York: Social Science Research Council, 1960). The discussion ranges outward from the factory as an organization and encompasses the chief functional areas of society. National Bureau of Economic Research, *Demographic and Economic Change in Developed Countries* (Princeton: Princeton University Press, 1960) is a collection of specialized and often rather technical papers on aspects of the relations between population and the economy. The "Introduction" by Ansley J. Coale provides an effective summary of the main points and questions.

Technology as an instrument of change has elicited renewed interest, perhaps occasioned by ecological and environmentalist concerns. A selection of semi-popular discussions from the *New York Times Magazine* has been assembled, with a substantial editorial introduction, in Wilbert E. Moore (ed.), *Technology and Social Change* (Chicago: Quadrangle Books, 1972). Moore dissects what Lewis Mumford calls *The Myth of the Machine*, the general title of a large two-volume study, the second volume of which, *The Pentagon of Power* (New York: Harcourt, Brace & Jovanovich, 1970) is highly recommended.

INDEX